GOLD TRADING

Why Investing In Gold How To Make Better Decisions And Learning Strategies

By

Gregor Kaufmann

Table of content

Executive Summary

The financial crisis of 2009 has seriously affected the world economy. On August 6, 2011, Standard & Poor downgraded the U.S.'s AAA credit rating for the first time since its granting in 1917. Developed countries have experienced an unprecedented 7.5 percent decrease in the real GDP. Meanwhile, the price of gold remains high. Just four days after the downgrading of U.S.'s credit rating, gold's price climbed to 1,800 US dollars per ounce compared to the average price of 1,224.53 US dollars per ounce in 2010.

This book is done in the interest of how gold should be invested, both in general and in the underlying circumstances. The starting point is to introduce the role of gold in the financial world and its features as an investment. After that, an econometric model is applied to figure out what the relevant factors are that affect the gold's price primarily. Considering the testing period from 1991 to 2011, with monthly observations, the findings are the following: the return of gold has a strong positive correlation with the change of the inflation rate; the return of oil is, to some extent, positively related to the return on gold, whereas the correlation is not strong; the return of stocks and the change of interest rates are proven to be not related to the return of gold.

Since the return of gold is independent of the return of stocks, these two factors, combined in a portfolio, will diversify the risk of each other. The second objective of this book is to estimate a proportion of gold investment in a portfolio including Danish stocks and Danish mortgage bonds, using tangent portfolios and another needful financial modeling in Excel. The suggested portfolio is to allocate 3.57% of the investment in Danish stocks, 7.20% of the investment in gold, and 89.23% of the investment in Danish mortgage bonds. The proportion of investing in gold should remain the same in the 2009's crisis, while the proportion of investing in Danish mortgage bonds and OMX20 should have some small changes.

The result does not necessarily mean that bonds are safer than gold and stocks. Bonds still have a risk of defaulting or being downgraded, especially under certain circumstances e.g., when the housing bubble burst or the credit rating was downgraded. To have a comprehensive conclusion, besides the recommended portfolio, it needs to be addressed that gold is a very unique asset, which has a static purchasing power to goods and services in the long term. Governments and central banks store gold as a backup for the paper currency. From a long term perspective, adding gold into a portfolio can enhance the ability of the portfolio to bear the risk in the crisis. The effect becomes significant when the risk of inflation and government default is an underlying issue.

Part One

Introduction

In 2009, the International Monetary Fund (IMF) issued the report of World Economic Outlook: Crisis and Recovery. According to the report, the world economy has been seriously affected by the financial crisis since 2009. Developed countries have experienced an unprecedented 7.5 percent decrease in the real GDP. Many economists consider this financial crisis as the worst one since the Great Depression of the 1930s. Large financial institutions suffered in the crisis. Banks were bailout by national governments, and stock markets reflected investors' lack of confidence around the world.

Meanwhile, the price of gold has increased continuously. On August 06, 2011, Standard & Poor downgraded the U.S.'s AAA credit rating for the first time since its granting in 1917. Four days later, gold's price climbed to 1800 US dollars per ounce comparing to the average price of 1224.53 US dollars per ounce in 2010. It demonstrates that the downgrading of the

U.S.'s credit rating scared investors away from the U.S. debt, which has been seen as one of the safest investments in the world. Further, people also worried that the rating could be lowed further within the next two years. To reduce future uncertainties, panicked investors choose gold.

Gold is traditionally considered by investors as a safe investment, especially during a time of recession with high risks of inflation, exchange rates depreciating, and bank collages. The main reason is that, unlike any currency, gold has an intrinsic value. It is a precious metal that is widely used in modem technologies. Historically gold was used as currency in old times. Even now it is still considered as the backup of currency for governments and central banks. The current gold price is indicated in terms of currency. And the current price of the currency is affected by the on-going financial crisis. Investors see more value in gold when they lose confidence in government bonds and the return of the stock market is negative.

However, this cannot completely explain the change in gold's price. The link between the financial crisis and the rise in gold's price is not consistent. The gold price itself is volatile. For example, during the boom period of 2001 to 2007, gold's price was increasing from 276.5 US dollars per ounce to 833.8 US dollars per ounce. This makes us think about what better explains the movement of gold's price. Is gold a better investment in the current financial crisis?

Therefore the purpose of this book is:

1. Identify the relevant factors that affect gold prices mostly.

2. Evaluate the risk-return performance of a gold investment.

3. Construct an optimal portfolio of the financial assets including gold, stocks, and bonds in Denmark during the financial crisis.

Why identify the relevant factors that affect gold's price?

The price of gold is turbulent from time to time. As mentioned before, there might be different reasons that affect gold prices, especially during the financial crisis. To determine what the real reason is for gold's price to increase, it is necessary to identify the most relevant factors leading to the phenomenon. Therefore, in the following parts, we will build a model including the most likely influential factors as parameters, these will be tested to determine which might affect gold's price. Further, we will also determine how effective these factors are. The results of the model testing are expected to have a reasonable explanatory power to answer the question.

Details of the model will be presented in Part Two of this book.

Why compare gold investment to stocks and bonds in Denmark?

One of the lessons we have learned about investment during the education in Applied Economics and Finance is the diversified portfolio. The portfolio is a strategy that combines assets with different proportions either to remain a fixed return, but minimize the risk of investment, or to keep a certain risk exposure, but also achieve the best level of return. In the period of recession, stocks do not make good profits as are expected. In this case, in theory, a portfolio combines with stocks, gold, and bonds could generate a better return and lower risks than a portfolio include only one or two of the three assets. In reality, investors do realize that gold makes good investments during crises, wars, or high inflation.

Thus, by comparing the gold, stocks, and bonds in Denmark, one could insight on the feasibility of a possible investment portfolio combing these three assets during the 2009's financial crisis, and how such a portfolio exactly would benefit the investment in reality.

The details of the model will be presented in Part

Three of this book.

Research Question

To sum up the previously discussed purpose of this book, the following questions have been formulated to guide the research:

What are the relevant factors that affect gold prices mostly? How they will influence gold's price?

What are the annual returns of gold investment in the last 20 years?

How an investor should allocate his investment in a three-asset category portfolio, consisting of gold investment, stocks, and bonds in Denmark before and during the 2009 financial crisis.

Assumptions

U.S. stock exchange, U.S. interest rate, and U.S. inflation rate are chosen to present the stocks, interest rate, and inflation in general.

Data on U.S. stock exchange, U.S. interest rates, and U.S. inflation are collected every month. The monthly observations are assumed to reflect the true market volatility.

Gold's price is present by the UK London Gold Price, U.S. Dollar per Fine Ounce.

Buying and selling stock exchange, bonds, or gold on the market has a transaction cost. Since the cost is relatively low, it is assumed in this book that the transaction cost is zero.

Tax is not counted when returns on gold, stocks, and bonds are calculated.

The model developed in Part Two might not have as high explanatory power as it is expected, as the individual variables defined in the model might not cover all the real factors. However, we believe that the explanatory power of the model should still be sufficient. Therefore the results of the model testing will be taken for further analysis in the book.

The risk-free rate in this book is set as the 3-month Danish interbank rate, which is taken from DataStream Advance 4.0 on 18-09-2011. Code: S01928 (Appendix 1).

Nykredit Mortgage Index is assumed to represent the opportunity to invest bonds in Denmark.

OMX20 is assumed to be the index of investing in the stock exchange in Denmark. Data of OMX20 is collected daily.

Investors are assumed to be risk-neutral, as they have the possibilities to choose risk-free assets to invest in the market.

It is also assumed that readers of this book have a fundamental knowledge of the capital market and financial modeling. Not all the concepts will be explained in detail.

Delimitation

The focus of this book is to investigate the gold investment in the current financial crisis for an investor holding a portfolio of gold, Danish stocks, and Danish bonds. Therefore the data of stocks and bonds are limited to the Danish market. The reason to set such a limitation is as follows: First, scholars are conducting a lot of researches on the U.S. market. As a student who majored in financial management in Denmark, it is interesting to focus on the local market, and see what results can be found. Second, such a focus also reduces the complexity of this book. It is well realized by the author that in the real world, a lot more financial products in diversified geographic locations can be included in such a portfolio.

It is not the scope of this book to build a model forecasting the movement of gold's price. The model testing, in its way, only assists a rational understanding of the phenomenon. However, if we have a large number of observations, it is possible to build an econometric model that predicts the future gold price.

Methodology

Research design

This study aims to provide a comprehensive analysis of whether gold is a good investment to diversify a portfolio. To provide a proper answer, this book is structured in two parts. One is to identify the most relevant factors that contribute to the turbulence of gold's price. The other is to determine how much a Danish investor can add gold investment into his portfolio. The structure of this book is illustrated in Figure 5-1.

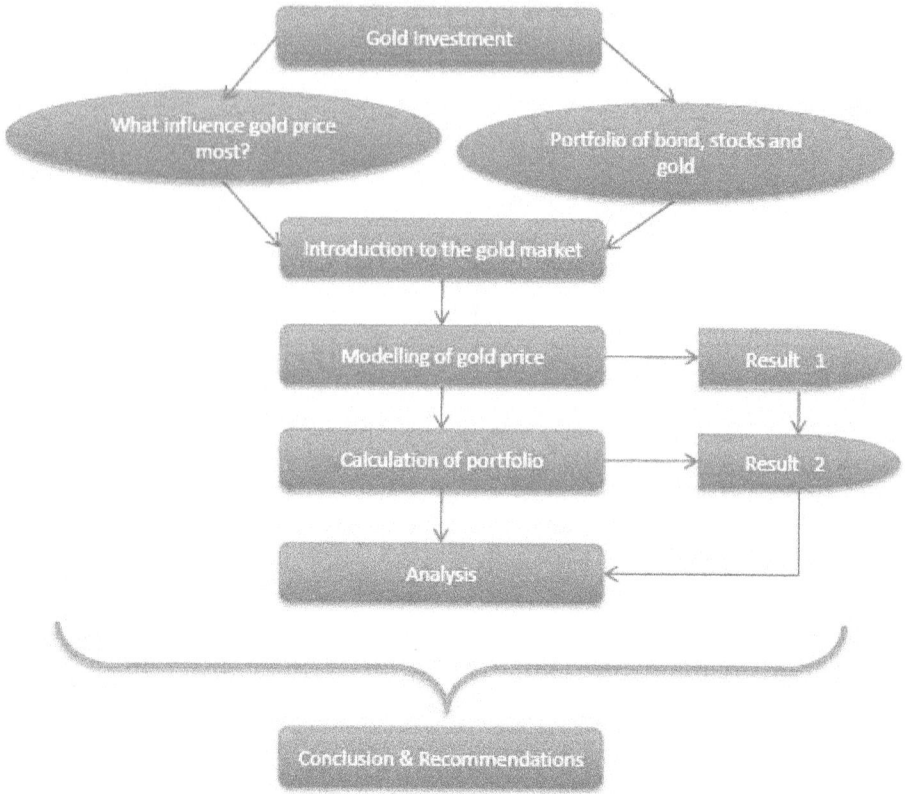

Figure 5-1 The methodological approach of this book

Three research questions are formulated to lead the research. To answer the research questions, first a section of _introduction to the gold market' is structured to present the characteristics of the gold market, and how it relates to the macroeconomics. In this section, the collection of data used in modeling gold's price will also be introduced. Second, the part of the modeling of gold price' sheds light on the rationality behind what makes gold's price changes. Since this part is to explore an explanation of a phenomenon, a deductive method of inquiry is applied. The inputs and arguments are drawn from different academic researches. Based on the inputs, a model of factors that affect the gold's price will be established. The model will be tested by econometric tools to investigate the relevance of each factor to the variation of gold's price. Results provided it will be carried on in the next part to pave the way for an optimal portfolio. The calculation of the portfolio can be a real case to validate the accuracy of modeling and provide guidance for investment in the real world.

Next, combining the findings and results both in Part Two and Part Three, an analysis will follow to link the results together and check whether theory and the practice can match and whether the model can guide an investor in making better decisions. At this point, the three research questions will have been answered enabling a balanced overall conclusion.

The approach of obtaining empirical data

In Part Two of this book, the empirical data for the UK London gold price, the oil price, the U.S. interest rate, the U.S. inflation rate, and the S&P 500 stock index are collected to build a regression model on how these elements will influence the movement of gold's price.

The reason to choose the price of gold in UK London is that it is one of the most influenced gold exchanges in the world; and it also provided the first digital currency of gold in the world, which gives investors easy access to trade on the market. Therefore UK London gold price is chosen to represent the investment opportunities for gold.

The reason why the major economic indicators from the US is chosen is that: first, the US economy has been the largest national economy in the world for more than 30 years. It also has the world's largest stock exchange, the New York Stock Exchange, and the world's largest gold reserves, and the world's largest gold depository, the New York Federal Reserve Bank. Besides, the U.S. dollar is the No. 1 currency in world reserves. It holds about 60% of total world reserves compared to the euro, which has about 24% instead. Second, the U.S. also plays an important role in the current financial crisis, which makes it a great example of the world economy.

In the calculation of portfolio in this book, a portfolio of gold, stocks, and bonds will be constructed. Data on bond and stock exchange is necessarily gathered. The portfolio will show from the perspective of investing in gold, Danish stocks, and Danish bonds.

Danish stock index, OMX20, is chosen to present the opportunity to invest in the Danish stock exchange. The index portfolio consists of 20 most traded Danish stocks listed on the NASDAQ OMX20 Copenhagen market, which ensures that stocks traded there are liquid and meet the requirement of portfolio theory.

The bond market in Copenhagen is quite big. It is among the top five in Europe measured by its turnover. The main investment opportunities in the Copenhagen bond market can be mortgage bonds, government bonds, and structured bonds.

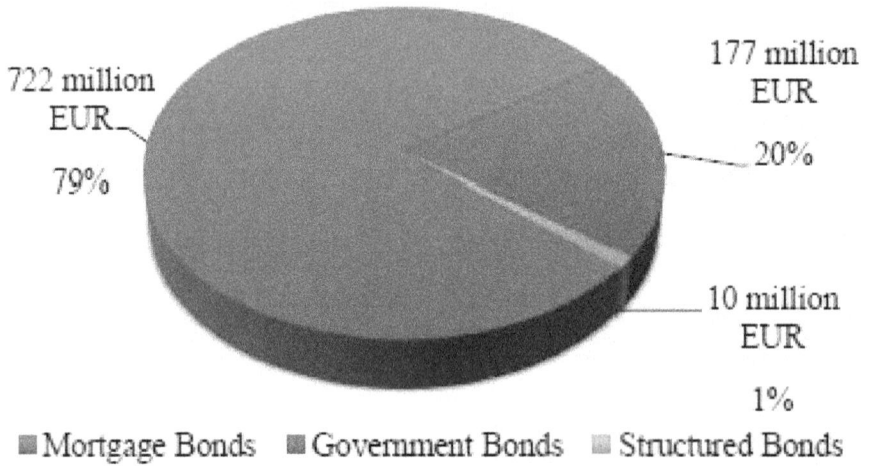

Figure 5-2 Copenhagen bond market value in 2007

As shown in Figure 5-2, by the end of 2007 the mortgage bond segment is the greatest part of the Danish bond market, counted for 79% of the market value. Therefore the mortgage bond is chosen to present the opportunity of investing bonds in Denmark, which means the effect of government bonds and structured bonds will be ignored. Nykredit Danish Mortgage Bond Index is the oldest index of Danish mortgage bonds. The index calculates a portfolio of the most liquid mortgage bonds listed on the Copenhagen Stock Exchange daily. It will be used as the Danish bond index.

The data of selected indexes are downloaded from financial institutes, i.e. NASDAQ OMX, Danmarks Nationalbank, Nykredit, the World Gold Council, and also from Reuters Datastream Advance 4.0. Statistical model testing and analysis are done by using software SAS 9.1. The calculation of portfolios is done using Microsoft Excel.

Literature Review

The literature drawn upon in this book can be divided into two streams: institutional theory, and practical guidance. The institutional theory helps to set the overall framework and provide a general basis for understanding the rationality for investing in gold. The practical guidance is used to assist modeling both in econometrics and the modern portfolio theory.

Institutional theory

In the field of gold price movements, many scholars have presented their theories on the topic. In 1900 gold was set as the single metallic standard for the U.S. dollar. It played an important role in the international monetary system. It was considered as a common denominator of different currencies and a principal form, upon which governments holding their international reserves. During the worldwide recession in 1958, the U.S. had a 4.2 billion US dollar deficit. Countries and central banks with a strong surplus in their balance of payments at that time sharply reduced their dollar reserves and increased gold reserves. In 1973, the U.S. officially ended the gold standard and allowed the U.S. dollar and gold float on the market. From then on, the price of gold moves up and down. When investors feel more confident about the economy, the price of gold normally falls. When investors grow fears of the economy, the price of gold normally rises.

Gulati & Mody studied the gold's price from 1972 to 1982, which was a period featuring large fluctuation in the gold price, and concluded that the main factors of impact are: inflationary expectations, exchange rate fluctuations, and changes in interest rates. In Jagerson's book, he explores that what happened between 2008 and 2011 to the price of gold reflected the consequence of the expansion of the U.S. money supply. Due to a large deficit, similar to 1958, investors and central banks fear the decline in the dollar's purchasing power, and therefore increasing the holding of gold as a haven. This is consistent with Gulati & Mody's finding that inflationary expectation has an impact on gold's price.

In Abken's study of gold price movements, he applied a regression model to investigate how the U.S. inflation rate and government policy affects gold's price. He found that a current change in gold's price was significantly influenced by the changes in its anticipated future spot price. However, the interest rate is independent of gold's price change. Similar to Abken's research approach, Lawrence examines the relationship between economic variables, financial assets in the U.S., and gold from January 1975 to December 2001. He concluded that the correlation between returns on gold and returns on equity and bond is lower than returns on other commodities, which confirms that gold is effective in a portfolio.

The role of gold in an investment portfolio is well acknowledged. According to Jaffe while gold is quite risky as an individual asset, its returns are generally independent of those on other assets. This suggests that gold can play an important role in a diversified portfolio.' Especially in recession and financial crisis, increasing gold investment to a higher level can reduce account volatility, and protect one's financial future in the long run.

Many empirical studies support the findings above. Lucey studied the optimal asset allocation by skew return and proved that in most cases gold bullion plays an important role in an optimal portfolio. Chua conducted a regression model of gold return and common stocks for the period from September 1971 to December 1988. He found that the gold bullion is an effective investment to add to portfolio diversification both in the short runs and in the long runs. By adding bonds into the regression Baur and Lucey tested whether gold is a haven in the financial market from November 30, 1995, to November 30, 2005. Their results showed that gold has a good hedge effect for stocks. However, the same effect is not significant on bonds.

Practical guidance

During the two years of study of Applied Economics and Finance, we have followed courses and electives in the program providing various knowledge and tools across topics and subjects covering both theories and practices. They are combined and applied in the process of writing this book.

Abken, Baur and Lucey, and Lawrence provide us with inspirations to construct the model to test what are the factors that influence the gold's price movement are. In Abken's study of gold price movements, a model had the gold's price movements at the left side of regression and the change in gold's price in the preceding month on the right side. In Baur and Lucey's regression model, the return of gold is regressed on the return of bonds and stocks. Based on regression, Lawrence added more variables to the right side. He included interest rates, oil, copper, zinc, aluminum, commodities, etc. By adopting the methods of these empirical works, the regression model will be the base of modeling in Part Two. Different variables will be carefully selected to be included in the right side of the regression. The period for testing will be from January

1991 to August 2011.

In the chapter on modeling, econometric models will be applied. Watson and Teelucksing defined that econometrics can be divided into classical and modern econometrics. The classical econometrics models include a single equation and simultaneous equations. The modern econometrics models include time series models, which explain the relationship between present and past values of a variable, such as exponential smoothing, ARIMA, vector autoregressive (VAR). Several chapters in the course of Applied Econometrics` textbook, Basic Econometrics by Gujarati and Porter, will be used as a step-by-step guide on how to run the model. The econometric analysis is done using the software program SAS 9.1.

The independent contribution of this book

To sum up, the existing research on the change of gold's price reported a lot of findings regarding the return of gold and one or two economic variables. But no study combines several variables, using the recent data to test their correlations with the price of gold.

This will be the contribution of this book. To extend Abken's study of gold's price movements more economic variables are included in the model. The testing period is up to date from 1991 to 2011 comparing to Gulati & Mody's studying period from 1972 to 1982 and Lawrence's from January 1975 to December 2001.

Also, this book will use the Danish market data to calculate the optimal portfolio to determine whether gold can diversify a portfolio, and use the findings to explain why gold is a good portfolio diversifier. The contributions of this book are summarized as to:

- Test the factors that influence the gold's price movements mostly from January 1991 to August 2011 including the price of oil, U.S. interest rate, U.S. inflation rate, and S&P 500.

- Optimal portfolio calculation on gold and Danish stocks.

- Optimal portfolio calculation by adding a Danish mortgage bond into a portfolio of gold and Danish stocks.

- Determine whether gold is an efficient portfolio diversifier.

- Explain the underlying rationality.

- Compare the proportion of gold in the portfolio before and during the 2009 financial crisis

Part Two

This part will be divided into two sections. The first section will give an overview of the gold market, and the characteristics of different ways to invest in gold. The second part will present a model and apply several econometric tools to estimate the factors affecting the gold price. A summary of this part can be found at the end of this part.

Introduction to the Gold Market

As common knowledge, gold is one kind of precious metals. The purpose of this introduction is to shed light on the role of gold in a financial word, and other features as an investment.

What is gold?

"Gold is a chemical element with the symbol Au and an atomic number of 79. Gold is a dense, soft, shiny metal and the most malleable and ductile metal known."

In ancient times the value of gold had already been discovered. People took gold to make jewelry and currency. It is a symbol of wealth, beauty, and heritage carrying memories and cultures. However, besides these, gold also makes significant contributions to a wide range of technologies. Due to its physical features as corrosion resistance and highly malleable and ductile, gold is being applied in space exploration, nanoparticle technology, and medicine. Moreover, it is also used as the bonding wire at the core of an iPhone.

Why invest in gold?

In the economic world, historically, gold was being used as a currency. It always plays an important role in the world's major currency systems. Gold first became the single metallic standard for the U.S. dollar in 1900 and the back for the U.S. dollar until 1973. After 1973, both gold and the U.S. dollar are floating on the market. Even though gold is no longer a monetary standard, governments and central banks are still holding gold as a portfolio in their reserves to back the paper currencies.

The price of gold has continuously grown since 2000. In Figure 7-1 the trend is clear. Even though there is turbulence during the growth, the price of gold in 2011 is approximately 6 times more than the price in 2000.

Figure 7-1 Gold's price trends from 1990 to 2011

From an investment perspective, besides the static price increasing, gold is very different from stocks and bonds. Stocks and bonds may face default risks if the issuer cannot afford to pay, but gold has its inherent value. To some extent, the inherent value ensures investor's wealth comparing to other assets. Also, gold has a more stable price trend in the long term. Figure 7-2 shows that in the last 20 years gold had less volatility than stock, which indicates a lower market risk. Therefore gold is one of the fundamental assets within any long-term investment portfolio to keep the value and lower the risk on the market.

The reasons driving the interest in gold investing can be summed up as portfolio diversification, inflation hedge, currency hedge, and risk management.

Gold and S&P 500 annualized standard deviation

(22-day rolling standard deviation of daily return)

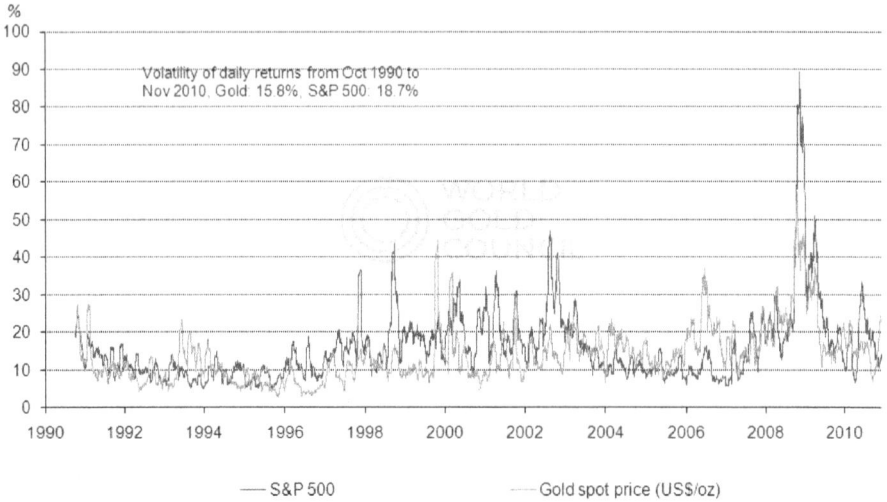

Figure 7-2 S&P and Gold: 22-day average. Volatility - 1990-2010

Where gold is traded?

The centers for gold trading are located worldwide. The gold market never closed. In Asia, the main trading centers for gold are Sydney, Singapore, Hong Kong, and Tokyo. In Europe, they are London and Zurich. In the U.S. it is New York.

How to trade gold?

There are direct or indirect ways of investing in gold. One can buy physical gold, like gold coins and small bars, or one can buy gold mining stocks and funds, and also other financial derivatives. In other words, one can buy gold as real, hold it, and sell for real to gain or lose the price difference. Or one can also gain or lose from not holding physical gold but from the movement of gold's price. The distinction from either way is not always clear. The best way of making a choice when considering an investment in gold is to define one's needs and choose the best option.

In the following, several common gold products will be illustrated. For the whole of gold products and details, please refer to Appendix 2.

Bullion coins and small bars are issued by governments. Investors can make their choice across the world. The size standard of coins and bars varies from small to large. Price for bullion coins is mainly considered for its face value, however, for bars, the values are mainly the gold content. They are ideal for private investors investing a relatively small amount.

Exchange-Traded Funds (ETFs) and Exchange Traded Commodities (ETCs) are financial products of gold. Those are like stock exchange-traded around the world. The major difference between derivative-based gold products and them is that ETFs and ETCs are backed by gold bullion held in secure vaults, but others are not completely backed by physical gold bullion. The advantage of this investment is that it is relatively cost-efficient and secure.

Futures and options of gold are like the others on the market. Only the initial margin (a fraction of the price of the contract) is required by the broker. The feature can significantly leverage an investment. On the one hand, it can generate significant profits. On the other hand, it can also cause an equally significant loss.

Gold Mining stocks are the stocks of gold mining companies. They are traded on different US stocks individually. Hence the price of mining stocks is most affected by gold's price. It is a good substitute for investing in physical gold.

Major players

The gold market has several players on it. These players can have a significant influence on the price, and therefore it is crucial to know who they are and what role they play. In brief, they can be categorized as governments and central banks, institutional investors and funds, and private gold mining corporate.

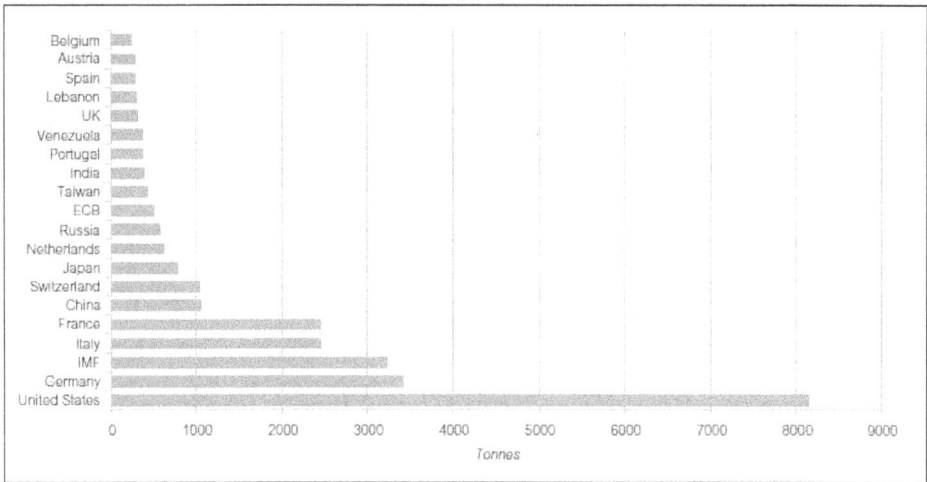

Figure 7-3 Top 10 official sector gold holdings (tons), as of September 2009

Governments and central banks hold capital reserves to back up their liabilities. The capital reserve, in general, is a combination of foreign currency, gold, and other kinds of assets. The percentage of holding each one changes over time. But the purpose of holding gold is quite similar to the private investors, which is to diversify the portfolio and control of risks. In theory, central banks should hold gold as a large position in its asset, so that they can be at a more safe position towards the reserves. In practice, this is the case. Figure 7-3 above shows the top 10 official sectors of holding gold. The U.S., Germany, and IMF are the three on top. One of the reasons that the U.S. is holding more than twice gold as Germany is that it is the biggest economy in the world. However, the current financial crisis could be another good reason. The banks that structure their reserves mainly on U.S. dollars will need to move more towards gold, to eliminate the risk exposure from
U.S. dollars.

Institutional investors and funds are very large. In general, they are one of the major players on the market, even though they do not sell or buy gold often. Instead of selling gold to the customer, they sell shares, which provide an option of investing in gold with lower access cost and more liquidity. They cannot sell the shares before they physically purchase gold, therefore their demand is based on investors' demand in gold shares, which has been growing constantly, and is believed to be continued.

The reason for private mining companies playing an important role in the gold market is to hedge the price of gold. They will detect the trend of price movement and accordingly hedge for the future price by adjusting supply.

Summary of characteristics in investing in gold

- Gold is different from stocks. The price of gold does not fluctuate as much as stocks. Like other investments, its price also goes up and down, but it is not threatened by inflation. As is shown in Figure 7-4, the price of gold goes together with the inflation. However, the occurrence of some big events which happened at the peak of the gold's price. The common of these events is that they caused the instability of the financial world, and the price of gold can reflect the risk and move accordingly. Therefore adding gold to a long-term investment portfolio can diversify the risk on the financial market.

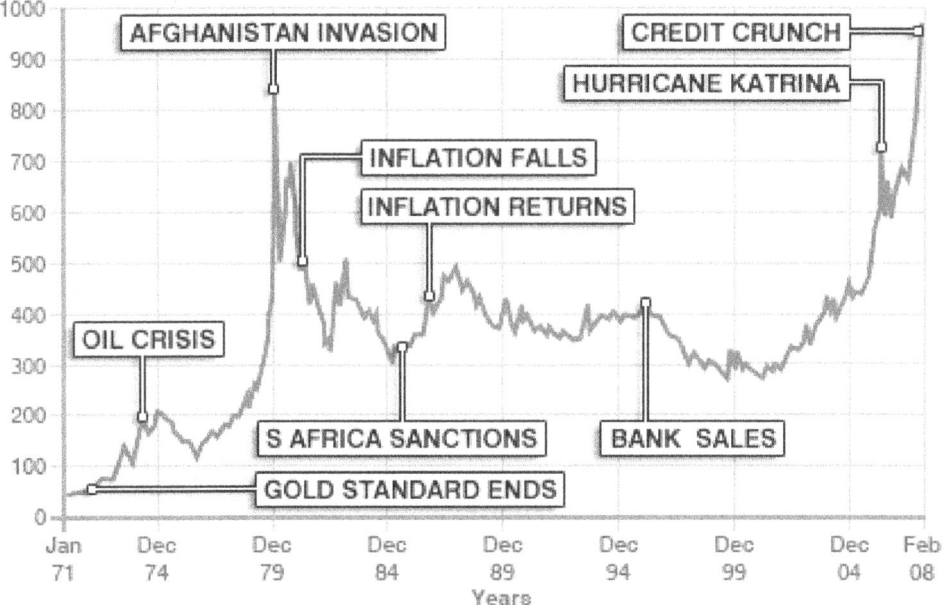

GOLD PRICE 1971-2008

$ per ounce

AFGHANISTAN INVASION

CREDIT CRUNCH

HURRICANE KATRINA

INFLATION FALLS

INFLATION RETURNS

OIL CRISIS

S AFRICA SANCTIONS

BANK SALES

GOLD STANDARD ENDS

Years

Figure 7-4 The historical moments of Gold's price

- No commodity has the same importance as gold even though in the short run it could grow more than gold. The key difference is that gold was a currency and still is backing currencies. This role cannot be replaced by any commodity on the market.

- Gold has risks. The price fluctuates from time to time. As Figure 7-4 presents above, the price of gold volatized in the past 20 years. If one buys from the peak of the market, the price may not come up again at the same level, the loss can occur. However, this is not exclusively happened to the gold market. Every investor will deal with the same in any market.

Factors affecting the turbulence of gold's price

Before building a model to test the factors that may affect the gold's price, the potential explanations will be gathered first. Later the model will be presented and explained. Different econometric tools will be applied. At the end of the section, there will be a summary of the findings.

An overview of what affects the gold's price

In McGuire's book, he argues that U.S. fiscal crises, economy, and inflation affect gold prices. U.S. dollar and gold can be considered as substitutes in an investment portfolio. If one wishes to hold more U.S. dollars, he will, therefore, decrease the hold of gold, visa verse. This is especially addressed in a situation that the U.S. dollar is not strong on the market. Investors fear of losing the value of holding dollars, in the term, they will sell the dollar and buy gold. Inflation has the same effect. High inflation risks the value of all kinds of investment. It, therefore, will also contribute to the price of gold. On the other hand, gold may perform better than other investments as it is the backing of currencies. This makes gold more attractive to investors.

The importance of the inflation rate to the price of gold is also reported by other scholars. Sherman, and Baker and Van-Tasse found that the inflation rate has a positive correlation with gold's price. Kaufmann and Winters reported the same result that the price of gold is dependent on, among other economic mechanisms, the change of the U.S. inflation rate. However, Lawrence concluded from his empirical study that there is no significant correlation between returns of gold and other economic variables, i.e. GDP, interest rate, and inflation rate. This finding is against the ones from other scholars, which makes the inflation rate an interesting variable to be tested in the model.

Jagerson and Hansen support McGuire's argument and also add three other factors as the fundamental factors affecting gold's price. They are interest rates, stocks, the threat of war, and gold supply and demand. As mentioned above, gold is an asset to invest in. Compare to other assets on the market, gold and the U.S. dollar can substitute each other under some conditions. When the interest rate of the U.S. dollar is low, investors will buy gold and sell the dollar. In contrast, if the interest rate is high, the opportunity cost of investing gold is high, the investor may rather hold dollar instead. It is the same as stocks. During the booming of the stock market, gold does not catch investors' eyes that much. As soon as the stock market collapse, gold becomes popular again. This can also explain why the gold price claimed again and again during the financial crisis from 2008 to 2011.

Nevertheless, according to Lawrence's empirical study, the stock exchange and interest rate are not related to gold's price, which leaves the space for these two factors to be tested in this book.

Despite the financial market disruption, the threat of war is another significant uncertainty for investors. During a war, the development of an economy is tremendously disturbed. Any currency may face the risk of hyperinflation. Due to the feature of gold investment, investors tend to buy gold for a safe haven. In 2001 after the U.S. invaded Afghanistan, the price of gold raised after a long time downturn. Again in 2003, the U.S. invaded Iraq, which accelerated the price of gold increasing one more time. All these reflect the investors' attitude toward their investment in gold. However, the threat of war cannot be quantified as other factors; therefore it will not be included in the testing of the model. But the effect it brings to the change of gold's price will take into consideration.

The balance between gold demand and supply has effects on price. The demand for gold shifts from time to time. It consists of three main sectors: jewelry, industry, and investment. Among the three, jewelry counts for 61% of the demand in the past five years. Over the past two years, the demand for jewelry has decreased, while the investment demand has increased instead. The supply, in the long run, is relatively inelastic, which means it does not change much even though the demand changes. The major supply of gold is from mine production. In 2007, 2,476 tons of gold were minded worldwide, while in 2000 the figure was 2,618. As Figure 8-1 shows below, the gold production level remains relatively static and did not have a great increase or decrease over the years. The production is slightly adjusted according to the demand. Thus the supply and demand of gold does not have a great impact on gold's price, and therefore will not be part of the model.

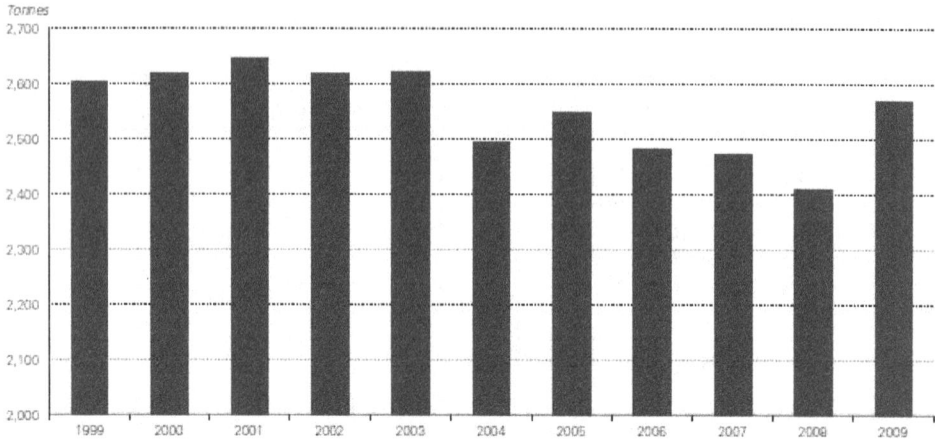

Figure 8-1 Annual world gold mine productions in tones

In Zhang and Wei's study of crude oil and gold markets, they found that there is a close interaction between the two markets. Gold and crude oil are the two main representatives of the commodity market. The crude oil price has a significant positive correlation with gold prices. The study period is from January of 2000 to March of 2008. Thus, the oil price is taken as a variable in the model. In addition to Zhang and Wei's testing period, the period is extended from 1991 to 2011.

Build of the model

To sum up, what has been discussed, the above mention factors will be some of a range of factors in the model. However, since the threat of war cannot be measured, it will not be included in the model. Also, the supply of gold is relatively stable in the past years; it will not be a part of the model either.

The variables are presented below:

G = Price of gold. Data on the price of gold is the London PM fix by month, quoted in US dollars. It is widely accepted as the benchmark price. For more details, please refer to Appendix 3.

O = Oil's price. Data on the oil price is _q New York Harbor No.2 Fuel Oil' quoted in US dollar per gallon.

INF = Inflation rate. Data on inflation rate is represented by U. S. Consumer Price Index (CPI) – All urban samples: all items annual inflation rate.

SP = Stock market. Data on the stock market is

represented by the S&P 500 composite prices index.

INT = Interest rate. Data on interest rate is represented by U. S. 3-Month Treasury Bill rate.

All the data above are monthly time series data from January 1991 to August 2011, as this period is where all the required data are available. Before constructing the model, it is necessary to check whether the data of the underlying time series is stationary. The main reason to do that is that: Firstly, non-stationary time series data will cause autocorrelation of the model, which leads to the wrong conclusion. Secondly, in a regression model, if both sides of the equation consist of time series data, the model often obtains a high value of R square, even though the relationship is not meaningful. Thirdly, some financial time series present the random walk phenomenon, which means the price today follows the price of yesterday plus a pure error term. It does not make any sense to forecast the price.

To find out whether the data in this model is stationary or not, the following tests will be applied: (1) Graphical analysis, (2) Autocorrelation Function (ACF) and Correlogram, (3) Augmented Dickey-Fuller (ADF) test.

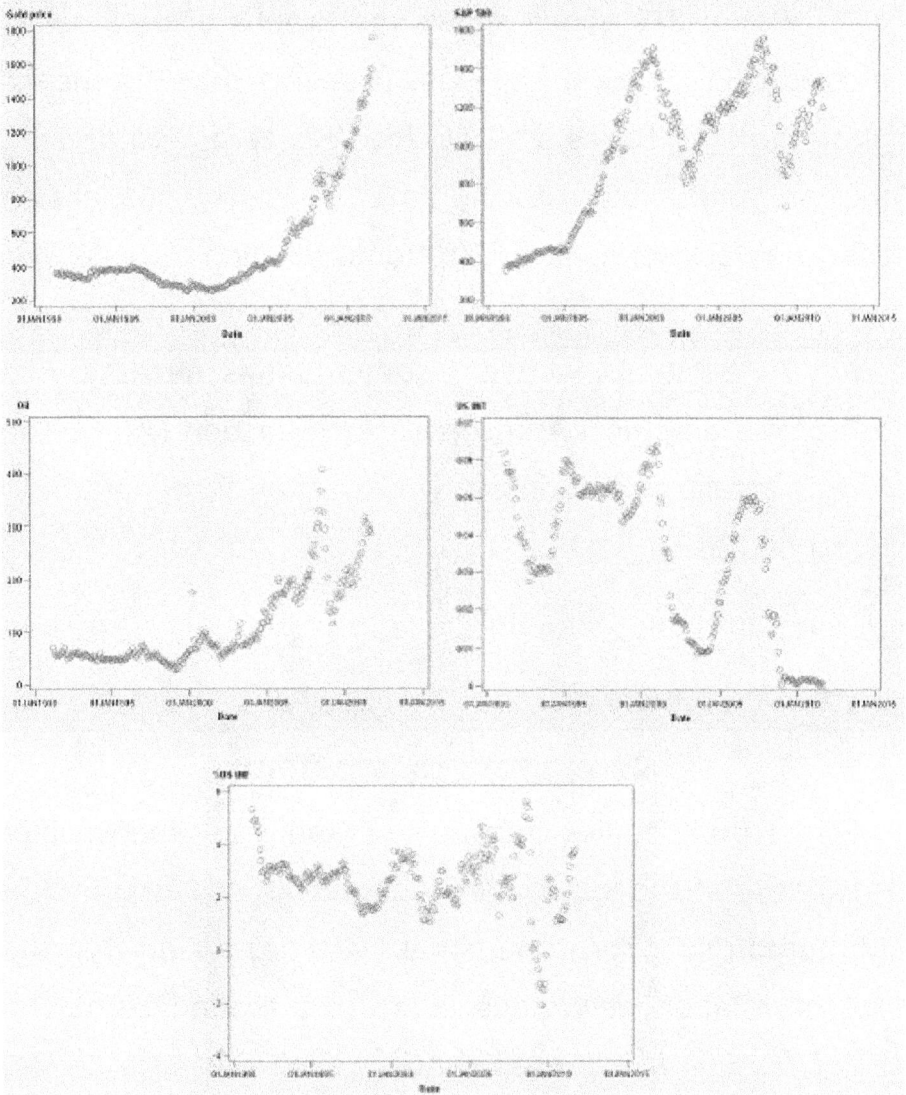

Figure 8-2 Scatter plot for data series All details refer to Appendix 4

Figure 8-2 above shows the graphs of data series plotted by time as the X-axis. It seems that the means of all the data series are not closed to zero, and present a clear trend along with the time series. The suspension that the data series is not stationary is high.

To avoid subjective judgment, it is necessary to perform a graphical Autocorrelation Function (ACF). The ACF is a test of stationary, which at lag k, denoted by, is defined as

$$\rho_k = \frac{covariance \ at \ lag \ k}{variance}$$

pk is a number lies between -1 and +1. When a plot against time the lag, we will obtain the ACF graph. The ACF graph of a non-time series date has a sign that the autocorrelation at various lags drifts around zero. The below Figure 8-3 presents ACF for all the data series. The pattern of a slow decline in ACF constitutes a sign of non- stationary. This applies to all the data series in the model.

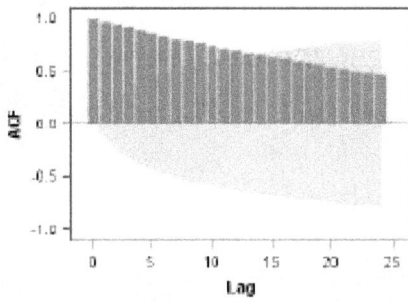

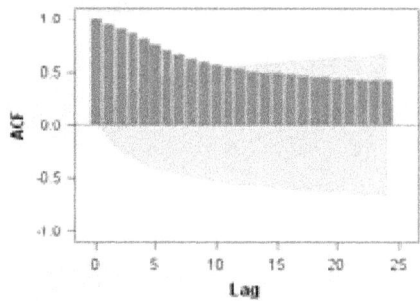

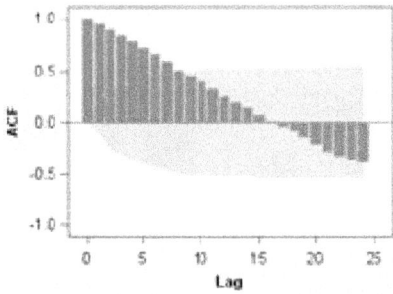

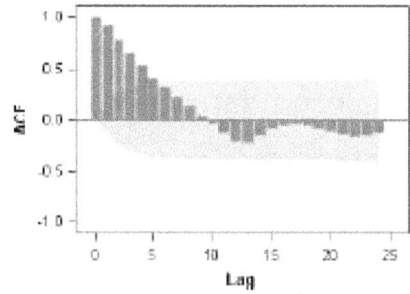

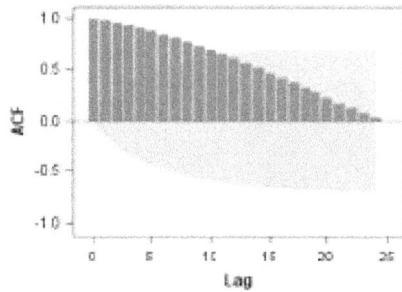

Figure 8-3 Graphical ACF for data series

Before making any conclusion, we will have a look at the ADF test (Table 8-1 ADF test for data series). The null hypothesis of the Augmented Dickey-Fuller t-test is

$$H_0: \theta = 0$$

meaning that by testing the regression:

$$\Delta Y_t = \beta_1 + \beta_2 t + \theta Y_{t-1} + \sum_{i=1}^{m} \alpha_i \Delta Y_{t-i} + \varepsilon_t$$

analyzed data needs to be appropriately transformed to make it stationary.

Table 8-1 ADF test for data series

Augmented Dickey-Fuller Unit Root Tests							
		For Gold		For Oil		For US Inflation	
Type	Lags	Tau	Pr < Tau	Tau	Pr < Tau	Tau	Pr < Tau
A Unit Root Without Drift	0	6.23	0.9999	0.10	0.7125	-1.76	0.0741
	1	5.14	0.9999	0.31	0.7753	-2.01	0.0433
	2	5.29	0.9999	0.14	0.7248	-1.73	0.0789
A Unit Root With Drift	0	6.15	0.9999	-0.95	0.7697	-3.57	0.0073
	1	5.29	0.9999	-0.76	0.8288	-4.79	0.0001
	2	5.58	0.9999	-0.97	0.7650	-4.11	0.0012
A Unit Root With Drift around a deterministic trend	0	3.43	0.9999	-3.04	0.1242	-3.35	0.0611
	1	3.02	0.9999	-2.73	0.2246	-4.77	0.0007
	2	3.42	0.9999	-3.02	0.1295	-4.02	0.0093

Augmented Dickey-Fuller Unit Root Tests					
		SP 500		US Interest rate	
Type	Lags	Tau	Pr < Tau	Tau	Pr < Tau
A Unit Root Without Drift	0	0.47	0.8156	-2.00	0.0439
	1	0.45	0.8116	-1.69	0.0863
	2	0.45	0.8100	-1.53	0.1174
A Unit Root With Drift	0	-1.72	0.4196	-0.89	0.7897
	1	-1.76	0.3998	-1.04	0.7374
	2	-1.70	0.4318	-1.35	0.6082
A Unit Root With Drift around a deterministic trend	0	-1.55	0.8093	-1.21	0.9053
	1	-1.58	0.7986	-1.50	0.8278
	2	-1.54	0.8128	-1.94	0.6331

The result of the ADF test shows that all the P values of gold, oil, SP 500, and U.S. interest rate are not bigger than 0.05, which is the significant level chosen. It means the null hypothesis cannot be rejected, that is, the analyzed data needs to be appropriately transformed to make it stationary. The P-value of U.S. inflation indicates that in the case of a unit root with drift, the null hypothesis can be rejected. However, in the case of a united root without drift and a united root with drift around a deterministic trend, the null hypothesis cannot be rejected. Since all the original data series in the model is concluded non-stationary, an appropriate transformation of the time series is required. In econometrics, it is common to plot logarithms of time series data. Therefore the following transformations will apply.

Return of Y_t (Gold, Oil and SP 500) = $LN(Y_t/Y_{t-1})$

Delta of Y_t (US Inflation rate and US Interest rate) = $Y_t - Y_{t-1}$

U.S. interest rate and U.S. inflation will not be transformed by return format, as their original data is already percentage. All the data series will be transformed and tested by ADF tests again. The results show that taking a log to gold's price, oil price and SP cannot make data series stationary (For details please refer to Appendix 5). However, the return data series is stationary. In Table 8-2 and Table 8-3, the highlighted P values are smaller than 0.05, which can reject the null hypothesis of the ADF test that data should be adjusted to be stationary. Therefore the return of data series is selected to be consisting of the regression model.

Table 8-2 ADF test for return of data series

| | | Augmented Dickey-Fuller Unit Root Tests | | | | | |
| | | Return of Gold | | Return of Oil | | Return of SP 500 | |
Type	Lags	Tau	Pr < Tau	Tau	Pr < Tau	Tau	Pr < Tau
A Unit Root Without Drift	0	-13.55	<.0001	-18.49	<.0001	-15.64	<.0001
	1	-10.74	<.0001	-12.62	<.0001	-11.13	<.0001
	2	-8.05	<.0001	-10.33	<.0001	-8.55	<.0001
A Unit Root With Drift	0	-13.93	<.0001	-18.50	<.0001	-15.78	<.0001
	1	-11.21	<.0001	-12.65	<.0001	-11.27	<.0001
	2	-8.54	<.0001	-10.39	<.0001	-8.69	<.0001
A Unit Root With Drift around a deterministic trend	0	-14.65	<.0001	-18.52	<.0001	-15.89	<.0001
	1	-12.16	<.0001	-12.68	<.0001	-11.38	<.0001
	2	-9.51	<.0001	-10.41	<.0001	-8.82	<.0001

Table 8-3 ADF test for delta US Inflation rate and US Interest rate

Augmented Dickey-Fuller Unit Root Tests					
		Delta of US Inflation rate %		Delta of US Interest rate %	
Type	Lags	Tau	Pr < Tau	Tau	Pr < Tau
A Unit Root Without Drift	0	-10.34	<.0001	-12.31	<.0001
	1	-10.70	<.0001	-7.54	<.0001
	2	-8.27	<.0001	-6.17	<.0001
A Unit Root With Drift	0	-10.32	<.0001	-12.39	<.0001
	1	-10.68	<.0001	-7.59	<.0001
	2	-8.26	<.0001	-6.22	0.0001
A Unit Root With Drift around a deterministic trend	0	-10.33	<.0001	-12.37	<.0001
	1	-10.70	<.0001	-7.58	<.0001
	2	-8.28	<.0001	-6.21	0.0005

Since the price of gold is a financial time series data, and the time interval of the model is by month, the price at time t is likely influenced by the price at time t-1. Thus the first lag of gold price G_{t-1} will be put into the regression. Oil and stocks are the assets trading on the market. Gold can be the alternative of them as an investment. However, the switch of investment or the adjustment of the portfolio may take some time. Thus O_{t-1} and SP_{t-1} will also be included in the model. The scenario, therefore, can be represented by the following economic model:

$$G_t = f(G_{t-1}, SP_t, SP_{t-1}, O_t, O_{t-1}, INF, INT).$$

Regression analysis will be applied as it is the process of estimating the value of the dependent variable by the explanatory variable. The regression model will show how the dependent variable is affected by explanatory variables. In this case, it will be how the price of gold is affected by the previous gold price, the price of oil, the inflation rate, the stock market, and the interest rate. The regression model is established and based only on available observations. The regression model can have a single explanatory variable or multiple explanatory variables. Multiple explanatory variables are the right ones to choose here, as it allows multiple factors that affect the dependent variable simultaneously. It can also handle explanatory variables that are correlated, which might be possible in this case. Therefore equation 8.2.5 will be rewritten as:

$$G_t = \beta_0 + \beta_1 * G_{t-1} + \beta_2 * SP_t + \beta_3 * SP_{t-1} + \beta_4 * O_t + \beta_5 * O_{t-1} + \beta_6 * \text{delta } INF_t + \beta_7 * \text{delta } INT_t + \epsilon.$$

Where $\beta0$ is the intercept, $\beta1$, $\beta2$, $\beta3$, $\beta4$, $\beta5$, $\beta6$, $\beta7$, are parameter associated with G_{t-1}, SP, SP_{t-1}, 0, 0_{t-1}, $deltaINF_t$, $deltaINT_t$ respectively. ϵ is an error term, which cannot be included as an explanatory variable.

Experiment and findings

The return data series will be tested and presented in this section. It presents the return of gold on the left side of the equation, and the return of stocks, oil, and the lagged return of gold, the delta of interest rate, and the delta of the inflation rate. The intuition behind is whether the return of gold is linked to these factors, or in other words, whether these are the major factors that influence the return of investing in gold. Also, since gold, oil, and stocks are the large markets for investment, investors may switch from one to the other if one market drops tremendously. However, this would not be possible to occur in the same period, instead, what happens in one market now may impact on the other market one period after. Therefore in the model, the lag of various explanatory variables will also be brought in and tested. The purpose to examine delta data series of the interest rate and the inflation rate is to test the linkage between the price of gold and the change (of difference) of gold and change of the interest rate and the inflation rate.

Experiment on return data series

Different regression tests will follow to identify the one with the most explanatory power.

$$return\ of\ G_t =$$
$$\beta_0 + \beta_1 * return\ of\ G_{t-1} + \beta_2 * return\ of\ SP_t + \beta_3 * return\ of\ SP_{t-1} + \beta_4 *$$
$$return\ of\ O_t + \beta_5 * return\ of\ O_{t-1} + \beta_6 * delta\ INF_t\% + \beta_7 * delta\ INT_t\% + \epsilon$$

The output of the linear regression model is:

Table 8-4 Regression output for return model

Variable	DF	Parameter Estimate	Standard Error	t Valu	Pr > t
Intercept	1	0.00563	0.00226	2.49	0.0135
Gold return 1	1	0.05648	0.06500	0.87	0.3858
SP return	1	-0.06100	0.04725	-1.29	0.1979
SP return 1	1	0.05260	0.04662	1.13	0.2603
Oil return	1	0.03192	0.01867	1.71	0.0886
Oil return 1	1	-0.02173	0.01821	-1.19	0.2339
delta US INF%	1	0.02129	0.00586	3.63	0.0003
delta US INT%	1	-0.01239	0.00953	-1.30	0.1946

F Value: 4.55
Pr > F: <0.0001
R-Square: 0.1175

To read the output in Table 8-4, the P-value of all the parameters except the U.S. inflation rate is not more than 0.05, which is the significant level chosen (column Pr > t). When P-value is lower than the significant level, the null hypothesis can be rejected. The null hypothesis here is that: in equation 8.3.1.1 for the tested parameter the correlation coefficient is zero, $\beta_1 = 0$, $\beta_2 = 0$, $\beta_3 = 0$, $\beta_4 = 0$, $\beta_5 = 0$, $\beta_6 = 0$, $\beta_7 = 0$.

The result in Table 8-4 indicates that all the parameters in the model except the change of U.S. inflation rate are not the effects that might impact the return of investing in gold. Also, R-square is also quite low, which indicates the tested parameters only explain a small portion of the variation in the return of gold price. Last but not the least, Pr > F value is defined as the probability of all the correlation coefficients of regressors are zero ($\beta_1 = 0$, $\beta_2 = 0$, $\beta_3 = 0$, $\beta_4 = 0$, $\beta_5 = 0$, $\beta_6 = 0$, $\beta_7 = 0$). Since the value here is very close to zero, which is smaller than 0.05. Therefore the null hypothesis that all the correlation coefficients are zero can be rejected. It means that the explanatory power of this model is strong.

Restricted least squares

The regression test shows that the return of gold is not related to oil, stocks, and interest rate by having a p-value, which cannot reject the null hypothesis. However, some of the values like the lagged oil return are very closed to the board line. To be more precise, in this section, the model will be estimated under the restricted least squares (RLS) and the F-test will test the joint hypothesis for oil, stocks, and interest rate. The F-test is

$$\frac{(RSS_R - RSS_{UR})/m}{RSS_{UR}/(n-k)} = \frac{(R_{UR}^2 - R_R^2)/m}{(1-R_{UR}^2)/(n-k)} \sim F(m, n-k)$$

m stands for many linear restrictions

k stands for the number of parameters in the unrestricted regress

n stands for the number of observation

The null hypothesis is that for the tested correlation coefficients, they are all equal to zero, i.e.

$$\beta_2 = \beta_3 = 0$$

$$F\,(SP_t, SP_{t-1}) = \frac{(0.1175 - 0.1061)/2}{(1 - 0.1175)/(247 - 8)} = 1.54$$

$$F\,(O_t, O_{t-1}) = \frac{(0.1175 - 0.0969)/2}{(1 - 0.1175)/(247 - 8)} = 2.79$$

The F test has the F distribution with 2 linear restrictions and 239 as the degree of freedom. The critical value $F_{0.05}$ (2, 239) =3.04. Since 1.54 < 3.04, we cannot reject the joint hypothesis that the correlation coefficients of the return of stocks and the lagged return of stocks are both equal to zero. It indicates that they add no explanatory power to the model. Therefore it can be concluded that the return of stocks does not have an impact on the return of gold.

The same applies to the return of oil. However, the result of the F test for oil, which is 2.79, is quite close to the critical value 3.04. To clear the cloud between the return of oil and the lagged of oil, two separate F test will be estimated.

$$F\left(O_t\right) = \frac{(0.1175-0.1067)/1}{(1-0.1175)/(247-8)} = 2.9$$

$$F\left(O_{t-1}\right) = \frac{(0.1175-0.1122)/1}{(1-0.1175)/(247-8)} = 1.44$$

The F test has the F distribution with 1 linear restriction and 239 as the degree of freedom. The critical value $F_{0.05}$ (1, 239) =3.89 and $F_{0.10}$ (1, 239) =2.73. The lagged return of oil is not related to the return of gold; however, the return of oil is different. If the significant level chosen is 5% for the test, the return of oil still seems to have a relatively low explanatory power. But if the significant level chosen is 10%, the result of the test can reject the null hypothesis that the correlation coefficient of the oil return is zero. Thus the return of oil is proven to be related to the return of gold.

Test the assumptions of the classical linear regression model (CLRM)

To support the results generated above, the three assumptions of the classical linear regression model (CLRM) will be tested.

- There is no multicollinearity among the regressors in the regression model.

- The error term is constant.

- The error term is uncorrelated

The reason to take a curtail look at these assumptions is that if some of them are violated, the properties of ordinary least square (OLS) estimators may not be legitimately applied. The consequence is that the results of the numerical test are not trustworthy. And the findings do not reflect the real case.

Test of multicollinearity

The definition of multicollinearity is that there is collinearity among explanatory variables. It means that there is no exact linear relationship between variables. It causes the problem that coefficients of variables are not linearly defined, and their standard errors are large. Therefore the fundamental of building the model is in doubt and the result is in certain inaccurate.

In principle, the most obvious symptom of multicollinearity is when r-square is high, whereas most of the regression coefficients are not statistically significant. As a result in Table 8-5, this is not the case of the model. However, to be sure of the diagnosis of multicollinearity, eigenvalues and condition index are discussed here.

Table 8-5 Collinearity diagnosis

Collinearity Diagnostics										
Nu m be r	Eigenval ue	Condi tion Index	Proportion of Variation							
			Interc ept	Gold retur n 1	SP retur n	SP retur n 1	Oil retur n	Oil retur n 1	delta US INF%	delta US INT%
1	1.61	1.00	0.018	0.071	0.030	0.055	0.076	0.046	0.17	0.049
...	...	....	...	...	...	...	...	...	...	...
8	0.49	1.82	0.16	0.084	0.12	0.058	0.39	0.21	0.61	0.058

The rule of thumb is that: If the condition index (CI) is over 10, there is moderate to strong multicollinearity. If CI is more than 30, multicollinearity is considered severe. In the result above, none of the CI exceeds 10 they are quite low. Thus, it can be confirmed that there is no indication of near-linear dependencies in variables.

Test of heteroscedasticity and autocorrelation

When the assumption of CLRM, that the disturbance variance is homogeneous, breaks, there is heteroscedasticity. The OLS estimators can still function well if heteroscedasticity is mild. However, if heteroscedasticity is severe, OLS estimates are no longer BLUE. It means the t value, p-value, and F test based on OLS formulas can be biased and mislead erroneous conclusions.

Several methods are detecting the existence of heteroscedasticity (i.e.Goldfeld-Quandt test, Breusch-Pagan test, and White's general test). Breusch-Pagan test is chosen here, as the test is used to detect heteroscedasticity in a linear regression model. The result indicates whether the estimated variance of the residuals is dependent on the values of the independent variables. The reasons why not choose other tests are that White's general test does not rely on the normality assumption. It relaxed the assumption of normally distributed errors and therefore is a special case of the Breusch-Pagan test. Goldfeld-Quandt test has the limitation of depending on the correct variables and the number of omitted central observation. Therefore Breusch-Pagan test best suits the case.

The null hypothesis of the Breusch-Pagan test is that there is no heteroscedasticity. In SAS, the output of the Breusch-Pagan test is a special version of the Breusch-Pagan test, which is called the Koenker version. It is from a regression of residuals on the set of variables that you assume generates the heteroscedasticity. SAS does not have an interface of the test. The below code is used to generate the test result.

```
PROC MODEL DATA=WORK.SORTTempTableSorted;
PARMS b0 b1 b2 b3 b4 b5 b6 b7;
"Gold return"n = b0 + b1*"Gold return_1"n + b2*"SP return"n + b3*"SP return_1"n + b4*"Oil
return"n + b5*"Oil return_1"n + b6*"delta US INF%"n + b7*"delta US INT%"n;
FIT "Gold return"n / PAGAN=(1 "Gold return_1"n "SP return"n "SP return_1"n "Oil return"n "Oil
return_1"n "delta US INF%"n "delta US INT%"n) WHITE;
INSTRUMENTS "Gold return_1"n "SP return"n "SP return_1"n "Oil return"n "Oil return_1"n "delta
US INF%"n "delta US INT%"n;
RUN;
QUIT;
```

The output is presented in Table 8-6. The P-value of the Breusch-Pagan test is not more than 0.05 (the level of significance chosen). Therefore the null hypothesis of that there is no heteroscedasticity is rejected. This implies that the standard errors of the parameter estimates are incorrect and, heteroscedasticity is a problem in the model. The estimators of OLS are not misleading.

Table 8-6 Output of Breusch-Pagan test

Heteroscedasticity Test					
Equation	Test	Statistic	DF	Pr > ChiSq	Variables
Gold return	White's Test	54.17	35	0.0203	Cross of all vars
	Breusch-Pagan	16.75	7	0.0191	1, Gold return_1, SP return, SP return_1, Oil return, Oil return_1, delta US INF%, delta US INT%

Autocorrelation happens when a variable is correlated with its own either in time order or in space. The appearance of autocorrelation leads the usual OLS estimators apart from best linear unbiased estimators (BLUE).

To detect autocorrelation, the first is to use a graphical method. By plotting the residual again time we can get a visual examination. The left part of Figure 8-4 shows the residuals along with time. The plots are lying in line around zero, and not showing a clear pattern of either positive or negative autocorrelation, suggesting that the residuals are random. To see this differently, the right part of Figure 8-4 shows the plots of residuals against lagged residuals. The underlining plots cluster around zero on both x-axis and y-axis and distributed evenly in four quadrants, which is consistent with the previous finding of random. However, although the graphical method shows a sign of non-autocorrelation, it is still qualitative. A quantitative test, the Breusch-Godfrey (BG) test is used to supplement the final findings. BG test is also called the Lagrange Multiplier test (LM test).

The reason for not using the Durbin-Watson d test is that the restriction of the test is that it has is no lagged values of the regressand in variables. However, the model 8.3.1.1 does contain the lagged dependent variables (lagged return of gold, lagged return of SP, and lagged return of oil), which make it an autoregressive model. Durbin-Watson d test cannot determine whether autocorrelation presents in an autoregressive model. Therefore the BG test comes to the stage.

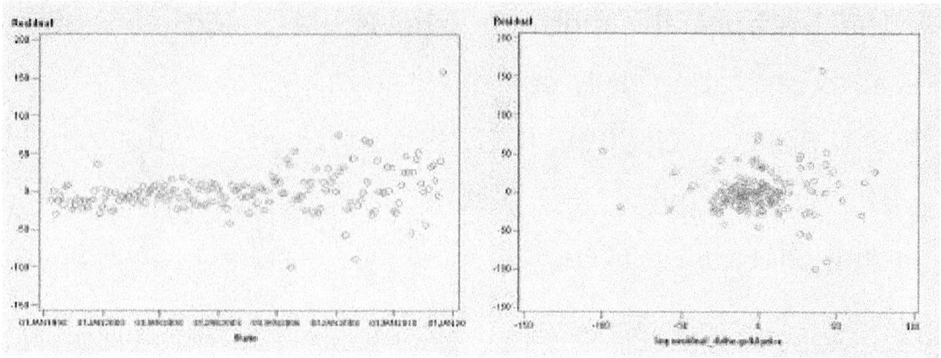

Figure 8-4 Residual plots

The null hypothesis of the BG test is no serial correlation of any order. The test statistic is given

$$(n-p) * R^2 \sim X_p^2$$

where, *n* is many observations; *p* is the order of autoregressive schemes, is obtained from the auxiliary regression of the estimated residuals. The result of the test follows the chi-square distribution at the freedom of *p*.

Table 8-7 Breusch-Godfrey test

Godfrey's Serial Correlation Test		
Alternative	LM	Pr > LM
AR(1)	5.3686	0.0205
AR(2)	5.3784	0.0679
AR(3)	6.2220	0.1013
AR(4)	6.5077	0.1643

The output in Table 8-7 generates four orders of autoregressive schemes. To interpret the result above, column Pr > LM indicates only AR(1) coefficient is smaller than 0.05, which means the null hypothesis, that no serial correlation display in the model, can be rejected. It is autoregressive in the AR(1). In the rest of the high-order autoregressive schemes, the null hypothesis of no serial correlation display in the model cannot be rejected, suggesting there is no need to consider more than one lag in the model.

In general, Heteroscedasticity refers to non-constant error variance, and autocorrelation refers to mutually correlated errors. In both of the cases, regression analysis will still provide an unbiased estimate, but the hypothesis testing (the t-tests here) and the standard errors of the OLS output are suspect. Biased standard errors lead to biased inference, so results of hypothesis tests are possibly wrong. To test the significance of the coefficients and obtain the trust in the results, heteroskedasticity-consistent standard errors (HAC) will be tested. SAS does not have an interface of the test. The following code is used to obtain the results.

```
PROC MODEL DATA=WORK.SORTTempTableSorted
PARMS b0 b1 b2 b3 b4 b5 b6 b7;
 "Gold return"n = b0 + b1*"Gold return_1"n + b2*"SP return"n + b3*"SP return_1"n + b4*"Oil
return"n + b5*"Oil return_1"n + b6*"delta US INF%"n + b7*"delta US INT%"n;
FIT "Gold return"n / GMM KERNEL=(BARTLETT, 2, 0);
INSTRUMENTS "Gold return_1"n "SP return"n "SP return_1"n "Oil return"n "Oil return_1"n "delta
US INF%"n "delta US INT%"n;
RUN;
QUIT;
```

Table 8-8 Heteroskedasticity-consistent standard errors test

Nonlinear GMM Parameter Estimates						
Parameter	Estimate	Apprcx Std Err	t Value	Approx Pr > |t|	Std Err	Pr > |t|
b0 (Intercept)	0.005626	0.00246	2.29	0 0229	0.00226	0.0135
b1 (Gold return_1)	0.05648	0.0883	0.64	0 5229	0.06500	0.3858
b2 (SP return)	-0.061	0.0504	-1.21	0 2276	0.04725	0.1979
b3 (SP return_1)	0.052601	0.0555	0.95	0 3441	0.04662	0.2603
b4 (Oil return)	0.031919	0.0174	1.84	0 0677	0.01867	0 0886
b5 (Oil return_1)	-0.02173	0.0192	-1.13	0 2600	0.01821	0.2339
b6 (delta US INF%)	0.021292	0.00517	4.12	0001	0.00586	0 0003
b7 (delta US INT%)	-0.01239	0.0109	-1.14	0 2548	0.00953	0.1946

The test result provided above in Table 8-8 seems that only rounding makes the estimated coefficients different. The more important is to look at the standard errors of the coefficients. By comparing the P-value in the tables it seems that the results do not change too much, which probably reflects that the heteroscedasticity and autocorrelation problems are not too severe. Oil returns become a little more significant, P-value is 0.0677 but it still needs the 10% critical level to reject a zero coefficient. The delta of US inflation was significant before and still is - even a little more. It strongly indicates that the change in the inflation rate is a factor that influences the return of gold.

Summary of findings

By conducting the above-mentioned tests, model 8.3.1.1 does not have the possibility of multicollinearity among the regressors. However, there exists the heteroscedasticity of disturbance variance and the appearance of autocorrelation. Fortunately, the problems of heteroscedasticity and autocorrelation are not severe.

$$return\ of\ G_t =$$
$$\beta_0 + \beta_1 * return\ of\ G_{t-1} + \beta_2 * return\ of\ SP_t + \beta_3 * return\ of\ SP_{t-1} + \beta_4 * return\ of\ O_t + \beta_5 * return\ of\ O_{t-1} + \beta_6 * delta\ INF_t\% + \beta_7 * delta\ INT_t\% + \epsilon$$

According to the model, the return of gold price is expressed by the return of the first lagged gold price, the return of stocks, the first lagged return of the stocks, the return of oil, the first lagged return of oil, the change of the inflation rate, and also the change of the interest rate.

The results of testing show that the change in the inflation rate is a strong factor that influences the return of gold. The bigger the change of inflation rate, the higher the return of gold is. The return of oil is also considered as a factor that affects the return of gold. It has a positive correlation to the return of gold. When the return on the oil market increases, the return on the gold market also increases. However, the effect is not very strong.

The rest of the elements, the lagged return of gold, the return of stocks, the first lagged return of stocks, the first lagged return of oil, and the change of interest rate in the model, are approved not one of the factors that relate to the return of gold. The return of stocks and the interest rate, in general, do not have a relation to the return of gold. The change in the stock market in the real-world should not cause or lead to the change in the gold market.

The positive relationship between the inflation rate and the return of gold is not a surprise. As discussed before, investors consider gold as a safe haven for inflation. Gold is not only a commodity, but it also has an inherent value. Even though gold is no longer a monetary standard, central banks and government are still holding gold as their back up of the currency. In 2008, after the collapse of Lehman Brothers central banks purchased total 450 tons of gold in the year according to the World Gold Council Reuters.

Gold, recessions and inflation

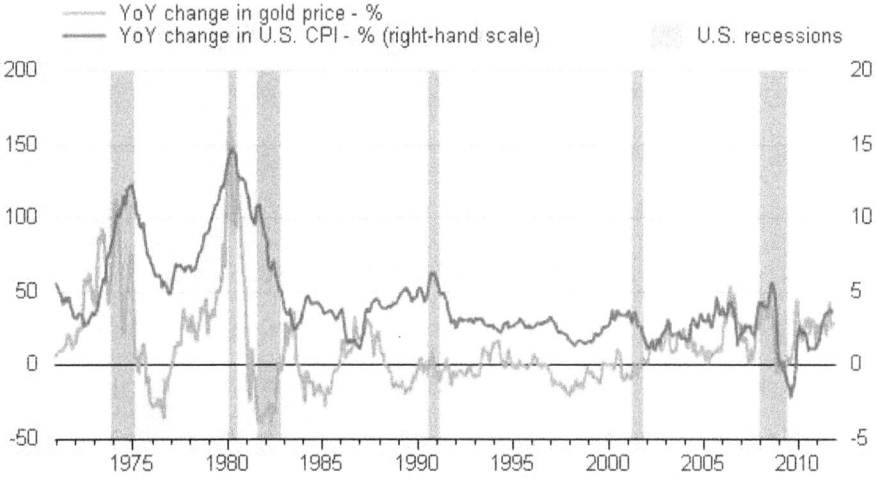

Figure 8-5 Gold, recessions and inflation

As an investor, by holding gold one can have a low risk of defaulting. Therefore when the inflation rate is high, investors tend to invest more in gold due to the fear of losing the value of the investment, and thus it increases the demand for gold, which leads to the rise of the price. Figure 8-5 above shows the return of gold's price and the U.S. inflation rate. They move very closely in the last decade. During the two financial crises in 2001 and 2009, when the inflation rate was high, the return of gold also surged. They have a clear trend to move closely especially in a crisis.

To sum up, from the empirical study in this part the return of gold's price is closely related to the inflation rate. The increase in the inflation rate leads to a high return of gold. Therefore Gold is a good asset to hold in times of the crisis, where the fear of financial systems collapse is high. By holding gold one can hedge the unusual inflation rate against the investment.

The return of oil also has some effect on the return of gold, whereas the indication is not strong. From the findings, it can also be concluded that neither the return of stocks nor the interest rate relates to the return of gold. The fluctuations in the stock market and the interest rate do not affect the return of the gold. From an investment point of view, stocks and gold can be selected as the assets in one portfolio as their returns are irrelative.

Part Three

Investing in Gold Together with Stocks and Bonds

The focus of this part is to examine the details of how gold can contribute to diversifying a portfolio. From the results in Part Two, it is proved that the return of gold is not related to the return of stocks. It indicates that a combination of both types of assets, in theory, can maximize return; while the overall risk is lower than the individual risk. Therefore, firstly we test a combination of stocks and gold. Later, bonds are added to the test to compose a three assets portfolio.

Besides these two constructions, the period of testing portfolios is divided into two. One is the overall period, which is from the 5th of January, 1993 to the 31st August, 2011 daily with 4867 observations. This period is determined by the accessibility of all the required data. The other testing period covers the 1st of October, 2008 to the 31st August, 2011 daily with 761 observations. The reason for setting up two periods is that in regards to the financial crisis people may consider a different situation than normal. During the crisis, a lot of assets generate very low or even negative returns, and the market (i.e. stocks, oil) is very unstable. In that case, investors are intended to be conservative and make safe investments, which leads to the change of their normal (long-term) portfolio structure. Since gold has less volatility than stocks (Figure 7-2 in Part Two), it is interesting to compare the outcome of 18 years to an extreme period. The result can recommend how the gold investment should be adjusted in a financial crisis.

In short, the structure matrix of this part is presented in Table 9-1.

Table 9-1 Structure matrix of Part Three

	Portfolio of Two Assets	Portfolio of Three Assets
Overall Period	General Portfolio (2A)	General Portfolio (3A)
Financial Crisis	Portfolio in Crisis (2A)	Portfolio in Crisis (3A)

Modern Portfolio Theory

Modern portfolio theory (MPT) is widely used in investment analysis. The concept of the theory is that instead of investing in only one asset, a portfolio of investments in various assets can maximize the expected return by a given level of risk, or equivalently minimize risk under a fixed level of expected return. Intuitively if different assets change value uncorrelated, or they are negatively correlated, the portfolio of these assets can have a lower overall risk than individually. However, even if assets are positively correlated, diversification can still lower the risks. In the previous part, the return of stocks and the return of gold are approved not to be correlated. Therefore, it is believed that a collection of both of them has a lower risk than either of them individually.

To obtain optimal portfolios, many mathematical formulations are used to calculate the result.

Return on assets: There are two ways of calculating the return on assets. One is the normal discrete compounding: $R_t = (P_t - P_{t\,1})$. The other is the continuously compounding: $R_t = log(P_t/P_{t-1})$.

In reality, the difference between these two mathematical methods is often small. Therefore in the following section, the continuously compounding for stochastic returns is used. The method is easier to work with when converting the daily return to an annual return.

Return on portfolio (Benninga, 2008): $E(r_x) = \sum_{i=1}^{N} x_i E(r_i)$

Standard deviation (Benninga, 2008): $\sigma = \sqrt{\frac{1}{N} \sum_{i=1}^{N} (x_i - \mu)^2}$

- **Variance (Benninga, 2008):**

$$Var_{(r_x)} = \sum_{i=1}^{N} (x_i)^2 Var(r_i) + 2 \sum_{i=1}^{N} \sum_{j=i+1}^{N} x_i x_j \, COV(r_i, r_j)$$

- **Sharpe ratio (Elton et al, 2007):** $\quad S = \dfrac{E(r_x - r_f)}{\sqrt{Var(r_x - r_f)}}$

A two asset portfolio:

- Portfolio return:

$$E(r_x) = w_A\,E(r_A) + w_B\,E(r_B) = w_A\,E(r_A) + (1 - w_A)E(r_B)$$

- Portfolio variance:

$$\sigma_p^2 = w_A^2\sigma_A^2 + w_B^2\sigma_B^2 + 2\,w_A\;w_B\;\sigma_A\;\sigma_B\;\rho_{AB}$$

The portfolios of gold and stocks

The focus of this part is on the portfolio of asset allocation between gold and stock. The mathematical and modeling method in this part is first calculating return, standard deviation, and covariance, therefore calculating the portfolio for both minimum variance and tangent portfolio for data for the overall period from the 5th January 1993 to the 31st August 2011. Further, we will make the same calculation for the data from the 1st October 2008 to the 31st August 2011, and then comparing the results in these two scenarios.

The data for the price of gold is UK London Gold Price found from World Gold Council from the 5th January 1993 to the 31st August 2011 daily. The stock price is the OMX20 index in Denmark from the 5th of January 1993 to the 31st of August 2011 daily. The risk-free rate is the average of a 3-month Danish interbank rate of the correspondent testing period.

The portfolios of gold and stocks from the overall testing period

The result is present below. From the 5th January 1993 to the 31st August 2011, the risk-free rate is 4.09%.

Table 9-2 Covariance matrix of OMX20 and gold from the overall testing period

Covariance Matrix – Yearly – Overall		
	OMX20	Gold Price
OMX20	0.05273	-0.00085
Gold Price	-0.00085	0.03568

Table 9-3 Statistics of OMX20 and gold from the overall testing period

Statistics – Yearly – Overall		
	OMX20	Gold Price
Return (Mean)	11.43%	12.64%
Risk (Stdev)	22.97%	18.89%

The covariance matrix in Table 9-2 is calculated using the macro function in Excel. The detail is shown in Appendix 8. Covariance measures the degree of correlation between two variables. In other words, it indicates how much two variables move together. Covariance is an important figure in portfolio theory to determine the degree of relation between two securities. If the covariance is high, it indicates the securities have similar movements and therefore lack diversification.

The covariance of OMX20 and gold in Table 9-2 is -0.00085, which is very close to zero. This finding is consistent with the result in the previous part that the return of gold is not correlated to the return of the stock. From Table 9-3 it is clear that in the overall testing period, gold has a higher return of 12.63% than OMX20 of 11.42%. The standard deviation indicates the risks of the two assets. Compared to the OMX20 risk of 22.97% gold has a lower risk of 18.89%. In principle, gold is a better asset with higher returns and lower risks than OMX20.

Next, both the tangent portfolio and minimum variance portfolio are calculated. Tangency portfolio is the portfolio that the Capital Market Line (CML) is tangent to the efficiency frontier. The efficiency frontier is a curve where each point on the curve is a possible asset location determined by the return of the portfolios and its level of risk. Any point below the curve is inefficient because the portfolio has less return at the same level of risk. The concept of efficient frontier is based on the assumption that unsystematic risk is possible to be fully diversified.

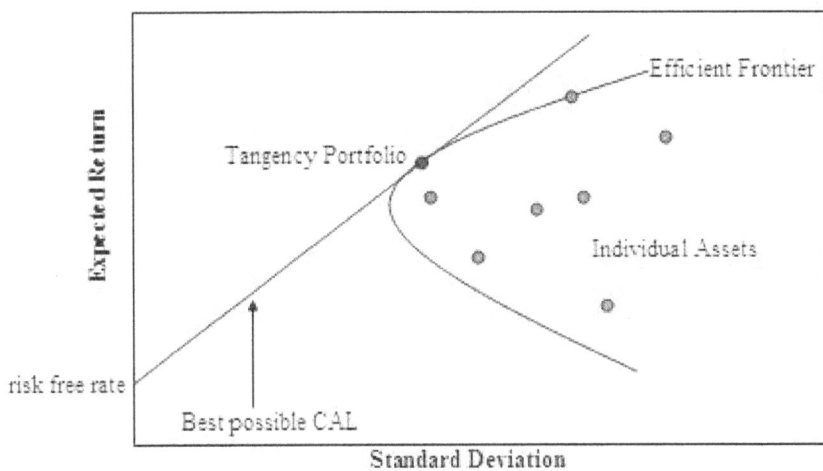

Figure 9-1 Efficient frontier, CAL, and tangent portfolio

As shown from Figure 9-1, CML is the line starting from the risk-free rate at the y-intercept, where the standard deviation is zero. It passes tangent to the efficient frontier, and the point is called a tangent portfolio. The slope of CML is called the Sharpe ratio, which equals the difference between the portfolio return and the risk-free rate divided by the portfolio standard deviation. The Sharpe ratio is used to identify the return of an investment for a specific risk. When the risk-free rate is the same, the higher the Sharpe ratio the better the investment is. It is because the higher Sharpe ratio gives more return for the same levels of risk. Therefore investors often use the Sharpe ratio to make investment decisions.

The following tangent portfolio of OMX20 and gold is calculated in Excel by using 'Solver' to maximize the Sharp ratio. In Figure 9-2 two conditions are placed in a screenshot. One is the sum of each weight of the tangent portfolio equals to one. The other is the weight of the tangent portfolio when it is larger than zero. The reason to use these conditions is that short sale is not allowed in this scenario. A short sale means that an investor sells security he does not own. A short sale is restricted in Denmark. According to the Danish Ministry of Economic and Business Affairs: With effect from 13 October 2008, the Danish Financial Supervisory Authority by the Executive Order on short-selling No. 1004 has prohibited short selling about shares in all Danish banks which are licensed under the Financial Business Act and traded on a regulated market. By considering the practical implications, all portfolios are conducted based on the assumption that short sale is not allowed on the market.

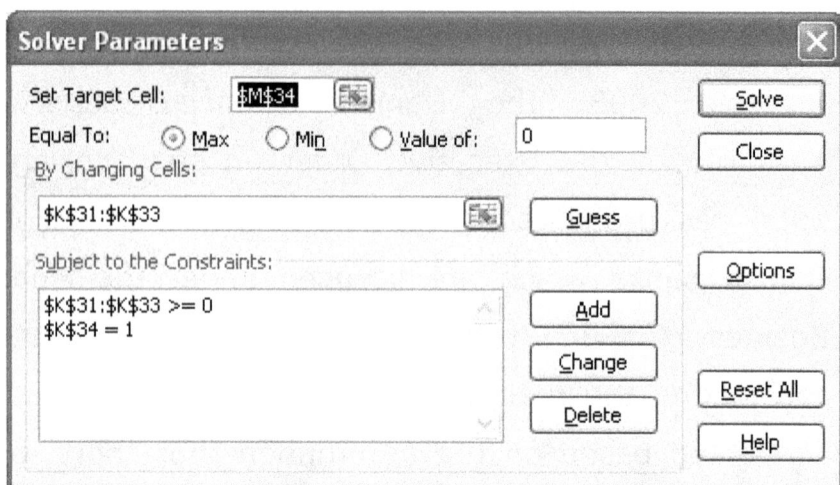

Figure 9-2 Screenshot of a tangent portfolio of OMX20 and gold

The tangent portfolio is presented in Table 9-4. It means that according to the portfolio, 37.1% of the investment should be placed on OMX20, and 62.9% of the investment should be placed on gold. This combination brings an expected return of 12.19% and a risk of 14.48%.

Compared to the performance of OMX20 and gold individually shown in Table 9-3, the portfolio of the two assets managed to lower the risks from 18.89% for gold and 22.97% for OMX20 to 14.48%. The return of the portfolio is 12.19%, which is almost the same as gold.

Table 9-4 Tangent portfolio of OMX20 and gold from the overall testing period

Tangent Portfolio - 2 Assets – Overall Period			
	Weight		
OMX20	37.06%	**Return (Mean)**	12.19%
Gold Price	62.94%	**Risk (Stdev)**	14.48%
Sum	1		

As is shown below, the tangent portfolio is the point where the efficient frontier and CML are met. If an investor only invests in stocks, he will have an expected return of 11.43% and have a risk of 22.97%. By diversifying the investment portfolio into gold and OMX20 according to Table 9-4, he can move along the efficient frontier and reach a higher expected return of 12.19% and lower the risk by 14.48%. Details of how to draw CML and the efficient frontier can be found in Appendix 9.

Overall Period - 2 Assets

Overall Period - 2 Assets

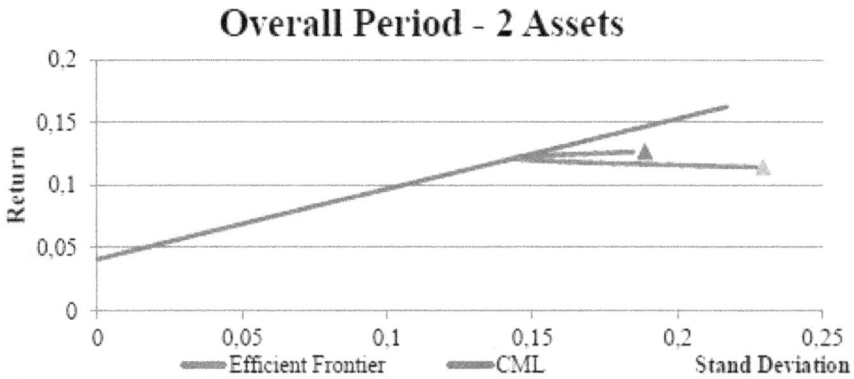

Figure 9-3 Tangent portfolio of OMX20 and gold

The minimum variance on the portfolio is a portfolio with the lowest volatilities. It is a point on the efficient frontier, which has the lowest risk. This portfolio maximizes the effect of diversification to achieve a risk lower than any individual risk level of assets regardless of the risk-free rate. In Excel, _Solver` (Figure 9-4) is used to minimize the risk in Table 9-5; the condition of the weighting is the same as in the tangent portfolio (Figure 9-2).

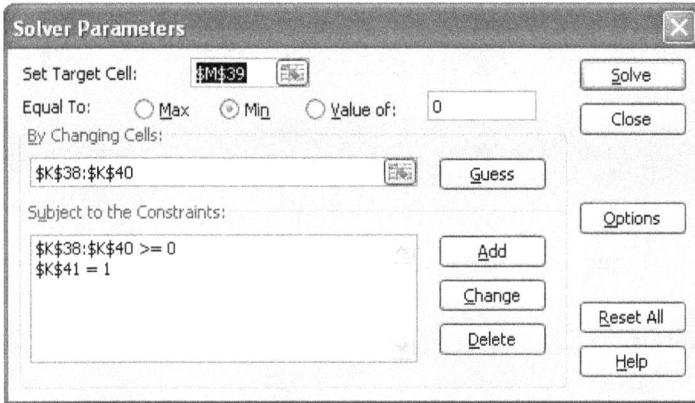

Figure 9-4 Screenshot of minimum variance portfolio of OMX20 and gold

The result of a minimum variance portfolio in Table 9-5 is very close to the result of a tangent portfolio. Investing 40.54% in OMX20 and 59.46% in Gold will have an expected return of 12.15% with a risk of 14.44%.

Table 9-5 Minimum variance portfolio of OMX20 and gold from the overall testing period

Minimum Variance Portfolio – 2 Assets - Overall			
	Weight		
OMX20	40.54%	**Return (Mean)**	12.15%
Gold Price	59.46%	**Risk (Stdev)**	14.45%
Sum	1		

The portfolios of gold and stocks from the period of the 2009 financial crisis

The current financial crisis started in October 2008. It has a significant influence on the global financial markets. Both the U.S. and Europe are deeply affected by it. The period is defined from the 1st of October 2008 to the 31st of August 2011. The average 3-month Danish interbank rate during this period is 2.11%, which is considered as the risk-free rate in calculation. During such an extreme duration both OMX20 and gold deviate from the normal performance. How different they are and whether we will still get the same result of making portfolio as expected to remain to be tested. The result is present in Table 9-6 and Table 9-7.

Table 9-6 Covariance matrix of OMX20 and gold from 2009 crisis period

Covariance Matrix – Yearly in 2009 Crisis		
	OMX20	Gold Price
OMX20	0.108824	0.002629
Gold Price	0.002629	0.066114

Table 9-7 Covariance matrix of OMX20 and gold from 2009 crisis period

Statistics – Yearly in 2009 Crisis		
	OMX20	Gold Price
Return (Mean)	1.10%	33.97%
Risk (Stdev)	33.01%	25.73%

The covariance between OMX20 and gold in the financial crisis is 0.26%. The covariance has increased compared to the overall period, which is -0.085 as seen in Table 9-2, though it is still close to zero. OMX20 and gold are still not closely correlated to each other even in the financial crisis, which means they are good to combine in one portfolio to diversify the investment.

However, the return and risk is a different story. First OMX20 lost approximately 90% of its return during the financial crisis. Recall the results from Table 9-3. In general, OMX20 has a return of 11.43% with a risk of 22.97% annually. Since October 2008, the return dropped to 1.1% with an even higher risk of 33.01%. The financial crisis badly destroyed the stock market in Denmark. The return is even lower than the risk-free rate of 2.11%. The high standard deviation indicates the big turbulence on the market, and therefore the risk has increased. Gold is different from OMX20. During the crisis, gold has had a higher return than under normal conditions, almost three times more than usual. However, its risks also increased by 1.3 times more, but it is still about 7% lower than OMX20. The overall gold is a better asset to OMX20 in a financial crisis with a much higher return and a lower risk.

By using the same method of calculation in Excel, the tangent portfolio is listed in Table 9-8. During the financial crisis, one should only invest in gold in a two assets portfolio with OMX20. This result is not a surprise. It is mainly because the return of OMX20 in the period is lower than the risk-free rate. Any investment in OMX20 will cause a negative rate of return. Therefore the investment in OMX20 is completely out of the question.

Table 9-8 Tangent portfolio of OMX20 and gold from
2009 crisis period

Tangent Portfolio - 2 Assets in the 2009 crisis			
	Weight		
OMX20	0.00%	**Return (Mean)**	33.97%
Gold Price	100.00%	**Risk (Stdev)**	25.71%
Sum	1		

In Figure 9-5, the efficient frontier for investing OMX20 and gold is shown. On the efficient frontier, OMX20 is placed much lower and further to the right than gold, meaning that its return is lower and the risk is higher compared to gold. The CML intercepts with the efficient frontier at the gold. It shows that the highest Sharp ratio achievable on the existing efficient frontier is to invest only in gold. In other words, gold is an absolute better asset to invest in during a financial crisis compared to OMX20. Though this provides a clear answer it seems somewhat extreme. Therefore instead of a tangent portfolio, we will take a look at the minimum variance portfolio.

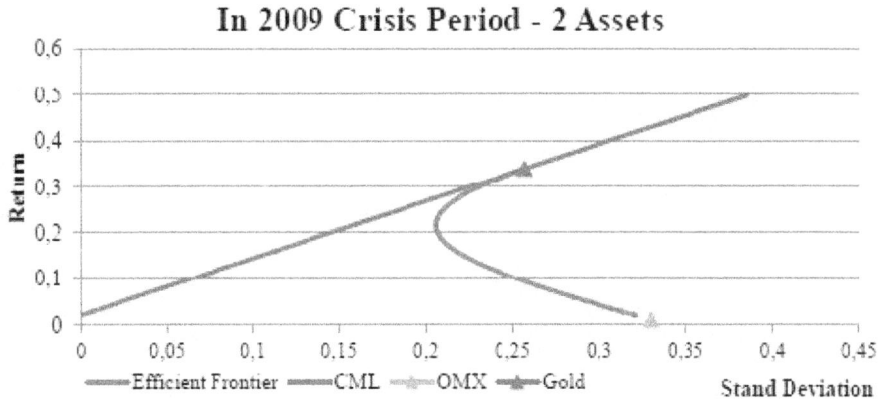

Figure 9-5 Tangent portfolio of OMX20 and gold in the 2009 crisis

Table 9-9 presents the minimum variance portfolio of OMX20 and gold from the crisis period. The result varies from the above analysis. To attain the minimum risk, it is necessary to invest in both of them, even though gold is an overall better investment than OMX20. By investing 37.41% in OMX20 and 62.59% in gold, the portfolio can lower the risk to 20.58%, which is approximately 5% lower than a singular investment in gold. However, with the decreasing risk, the return is also reduced by 12.3%.

Minimum Variance Portfolio - 2 Assets in the 2009 crisis			
	Weight		
OMX20	37.41%	**Return (Mean)**	21.67%
Gold Price	62.59%	**Risk (Stdev)**	20.58%
Sum	1		

Table 9-9 Minimum variance portfolio of OMX20 and gold from the crisis period

Summary of the portfolio of stocks and gold

To sum up the findings of investment in two assets, gold and OMX20, the construction of a portfolio is quite different during a crisis from the normal period. In principle, investing in gold and OMX20 as a portfolio is riskier during a crisis than in a normal period. The minimum risk of the two-asset combination is increased from 14.45% to 20.58% (Table 9-10). Overall, gold does not have a covariance with OMX20, which is consistent with the findings in Part Two that stocks do not affect the price of gold. Even though gold has a slightly higher return and litter lower risk than OMX20 in Denmark, by investing in both of them can reduce the risk of only investing in one.

Table 9-10 Risk and return of two - asset classes

	Expected return	Expected return in 2009 crisis	Risk	Risk in 2009 crisis
OMX20	11.43%	1.1%	22.97%	33.01 %
Gold	12.64%	33.97 %	18.89%	25.73 %
Tangent portfolio	12.19%	33.97 %	14.48%	25.1%
Minimum variance portfolio	12.15%	21.67 %	14.45%	20.58 %

The effect of diversifying the risk is even higher during a financial crisis. A portfolio of both assets can bring down the risk to 20.58% compared to the individual risk of OMX20, which is 33.01% (Table 9-10). Therefore it can be concluded that gold and stocks are both valuable to be included in an investment portfolio. They can provide an efficient portfolio with higher returns and lower risk. The effect of both is significant. Hence if an investor is more risk conservative, he should invest in a minimum risk portfolio. This portfolio is not influenced as much by the financial crisis, as it is aiming at eliminating the risk. Thus, there are no big adjustments needed. The portfolio during the current financial crisis is similar to the normal period. Though if an investor uses the sharp ratio, which considers the return with specific risk, gold should be preferred to OMX20 during the current crisis, as it has a better return with lower risk.

The portfolios of gold, stocks, and bond

In this part, a portfolio of three assets: gold, OMX20, and Danish mortgage bond (referred to as a bond in the following) will be calculated to get a more appropriate weight for each asset. Portfolios will be discussed for an overall period as well as for the financial crisis.

The data used to conduct the portfolios is the same as used in the previous part. The opportunity of investing in bonds in Denmark is present at the Nykredit Mortgage Index, which holds the majority of the Danish bond market counting for 79% of the market value.

The portfolios of gold, stocks, and bonds from the overall testing period

Both gold and stocks are finical products with certain risks. Especially the stock market has shown high turbulence during the crisis. As an investor, bonds should also be considering alongside stocks and gold. Denmark, particularly, is the second-largest mortgage bond market in Europe. Compared to gold and stocks, the mortgage bond offers a high degree of security. In history, it has never been defaulted, which is due to the extremely conservative regulatory policy of the Danish Financial Service. Below is the risk and return of gold, OMX20, and Danish mortgage bond in the overall testing period from the 5th January 1993 to 31st August 2011.

Table 9-11 Risk and return of gold, OMX20, and Danish mortgage bond

	OMX20	Gold Price	Bond
Return (Mean)	11.43%	12.64%	9.81%
Risk (Stdev)	22.97%	18.89%	4.39%
Return per risk	0.5	0.67	2.23

As is presented above, the return of Danish bonds is the lowest among the three assets. However, the risk of bonds is also the lowest. To define whether the risk is associated with the return, the return per percentage of risk on the bond gives a better picture. The number is calculated by return divided by risk. The higher the number, the better return can be generated by taking extra units of risks on the asset. In Table 9-11, even though the bond has the lowest return with the lowest risk; the return per risk is the highest. This indicates that for each unit of risk added on the bonds; a higher return can be generated compared to taking risks on OMX20 and gold. In this sense, bonds are a good asset to invest in.

How may bonds diversify the investment of gold together with stocks? The covariance of these three assets should be investigated to answer this question. According to Table 9-12, bonds have a very low covariance to OMX20 and gold, which is almost zero. The low covariance tells that bonds are not moving together with OMX20 and gold. Hence, bonds are a good asset to add to the portfolio to diversify the risk of each asset.

Table 9-12 Covariance matrix of OMX20, gold and mortgage bond from the overall testing period

	Bond
OMX20	0.00047
Gold Price	0.000079

Similar to the two-asset portfolio, both the tangent portfolio (Table 9-13) and the minimum variance portfolio (Table 9-14) are calculated. Due to the low risk and relatively high return, bonds dominate the majority of the portfolio. OMX20 and gold together count for approximately 10 percent. The result is not surprising, as the return per risk among three assets, bonds is the highest. For each unit of risk an investor bears, a bond gives the best return. Therefore it is preferable to OMX20 and gold.

Table 9-13 Tangent portfolio of OMX20, gold and bonds from the overall testing period

Weight		Return (Mean)	10.07%
OMX20 20	3.57%		
Gold Price	7.20%		
Bond	89.23%	Risk (Stdev)	4.27%
Sum	1		

Table 9-14 Minimum variance portfolio of OMX20, gold and bonds from the overall period

Weight		Return (Mean)	9.99%
OMX20 20	2.67%		
Gold Price	4.91%		
Bond	92.42%	Risk (Stdev)	4.24%
Sum	1		

Compared to the two-asset portfolio (Table 9-4 and Table 9-5), the contribution of bonds brings the risk of the portfolio is almost halved, compared to the portfolio consisting only of gold and OMX20. At the same time, OMX20 and bonds diversify the risk of bond and bring a slightly higher return than bonds itself. However, the effect is not much. In the following figure, gold and OMX20 are placed far to the left showing a higher risk (standard deviation). The point of intersection between the efficient frontier and CML are much closer to that of bonds, compared to stocks and gold, see the figure below. It is consistent with the tangent portfolio. It can be seen in Figure 9-6 below that the vertical distance between the three points is very little, whereas the horizontal distance is much larger, This translates into a similar return on the three asserts, whereas there is a gap between the risk. Thus the tangent portfolio includes a high percentage of bonds, which diminish the ability of gold and OMX20 to diversify the portfolio.

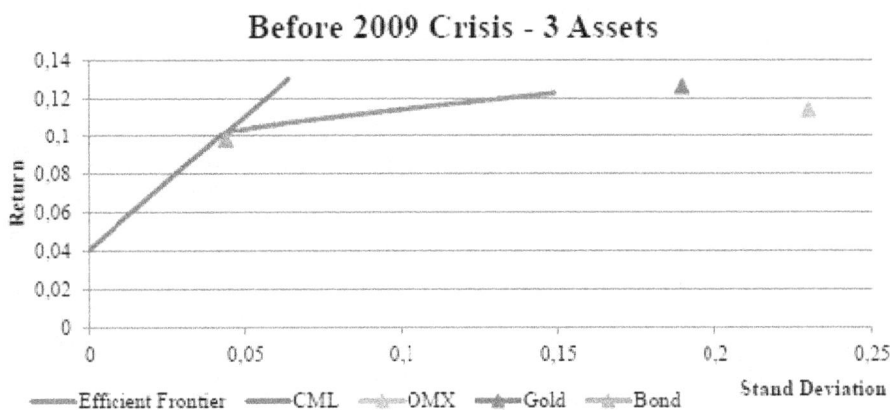

Figure 9-6 Tangent portfolio of OMX20, gold, and bond

The portfolios of gold, stocks, and bonds from the period of the financial crisis

The financial crisis has had a large impact on the return of OMX20 and gold. However, it is not the case for bonds. The Danish mortgage bond played even better with a higher return and lower risk than the overall period (Table 9-15). One of the reasons that Danish mortgage bonds are attractive is that the security behind them is very high due to the Danish legislation as well as the credit policies of Danish mortgage banks. The covariance of bond and gold stays the same. But the covariance of bond and OMX20 has changed to a negative relationship (Table 9-16). It is not a surprise from an investment in the point of view, as the lower return of OMX20 leads the investors to switch to a better asset with stable return and low default risk.

Since the performance of bonds is quite stable, the portfolios during the crisis should be more or less the same as the overall period. The tangent portfolio in Table 9-17 suggests that to achieve a portfolio with a maximized Sharpe ratio; one should invest 99.44% in bonds, 7.14% in gold, and only 0.42% in OMX20. The decreased percentage of OMX20 stocks in the portfolio during the crisis (3.57% before the crisis in Table 9-13) reflects the fact that OMX20 has a much higher than normal risk of 33.01% and a very low return of 1.1%, which is even lower than the risk-free rate of 2.11%. It means that leaving the money in the bank is a better investment than investing in OMX20 during the crisis period. Gold stays at the same investment level, not much change. The return of the tangent portfolio is 2.58% higher during the crisis, whereas the risk is slightly lower. This is mainly due to the good performance of bonds. OMX20 is not a good asset during the crisis. The investment in gold has proved to remain at the same level.

Table 9-15 Risk and return of gold, OMX20 20 and bonds in 2009 crisis

	OMX20	Gold Price	Bond
Return (Mean)	1.10%	33.97%	11.05%
Risk (Stdev)	33.01%	25.73%	3.83%

Table 9-16 Covariance matrix of OMX20, gold and bonds in 2009 crisis

	Bond
OMX20 20	-0.00087
Gold Price	0.00010

If the aim is to eliminate the risk on the investment, the minimum variance portfolio shows the right picture. Table 9-18 shows the preferred minimum variance portfolio chosen during a crisis. The interesting point is that the percentage invested in OMX20 stocks remains at the same. However, the proportion of gold is reduced from 4.91% (Table 9-14) to 1.88%. The minimum risk (3.73% in Table 9-18) that can be achieved in the crisis is lower than in general (4.24% in Table 9-14). The reason for that is because during the crisis the return of OMX20 stocks is negatively related to the return of the bonds, but the return of gold is positively related. In that sense, OMX20 is a better diversifying asset than gold to bring down the risk of the bonds, thus to reach the minimum risk.

Table 9-17 Tangent portfolio of OMX20, gold and bond in crisis

Weight			
OMX20	0.42%	Return (Mean)	12.65%
Gold Price	7.14%		
Bond	92.44%	Risk (Stdev)	3.99%
Sum	1		

Table 9-18 Minimum variance portfolio of OMX20, gold and bond in crisis

Weight			
OMX20	2.00%	Return (Mean)	11.28%
Gold Price	1.88%		
Bond	96.12%	Risk (Stdev)	3.73%
Sum	1		

Even though both the tangent portfolio and the minimum variance portfolio are presenting in both the two-asset portfolio and three-asset portfolio. In the real world, tangent the portfolio is chosen by most investors as it optimizes the return and risk. Whereas the minimum variance portfolio only focuses on achieving the lowest risk regardless of the return, therefore it is less popular. However, it gives a good approximation of the minimum risk achievable on a given portfolio, especially in comparison to different periods. This tells us that it is possible to invest in a portfolio with lower risk during the crisis, as long as one of the assets in the portfolio is proficiently better than the others.

Summary of the portfolio of gold, stocks and mortgage bond

In the previous part, we analyzed a portfolio consisting of gold and OMX20. The analysis showed that investment in gold can diversify the risk of investing in stocks. The effect proved to be even higher during the crisis. However, when the Danish mortgage bond is added into the portfolio, the picture changes radically. Table 9-19 below lists the expected return of both individual assets and the combined portfolio. Even though the bonds have a slightly lower return compared to gold and stocks, the risk is significantly lower.

Table 9-19 Risk and return of three assets classes

	Expected return	Expected return in crisis	Risk	Risk in crisis
OMX20 20	11.43%	1.1%	22.97%	33.01%
Gold	12.64%	33.9 7%	18.89%	25.73%
Bond	9.81%	11.0 5%	4.39%	3.83%
Tangent portfolio	10.7%	12.6 5%	4.27%	4.24%
Minimum variance portfolio	9.99%	11.2 8%	3.99%	3.73%

How gold, Danish mortgage bond, and OMX20 perform differently is illustrated in Figure 9-7 and Figure 9-8. The X-axis stands for the risk. The Y-axis stands for the excess return from the risk-free rate. The longer the line on the X-axis, the higher the risk is for the asset. Whereas, the higher the line towards the Y-axis, the higher the excess return is. The slope of each line indicates the return per unit risk. The asset with a steeper slope has a better return per unit risk than the one with a flatter slope.

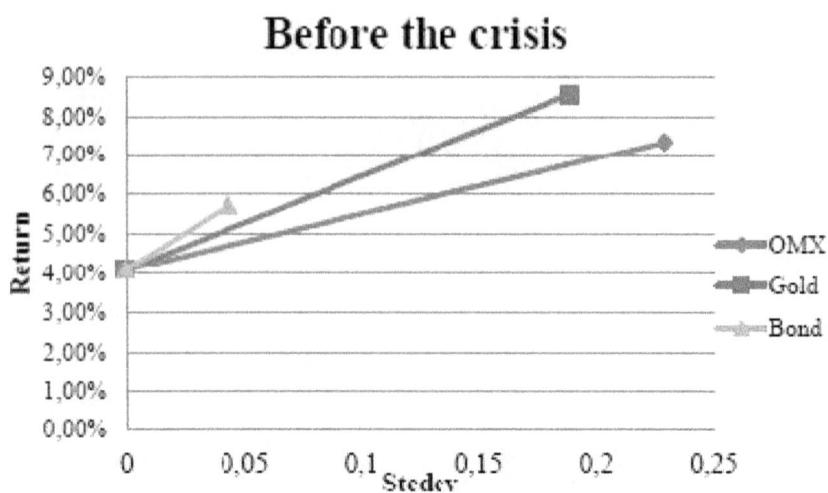

Figure 9-7 Assets performance before the 2009 crisis

Before the 2009 crisis (Figure 9-7), gold has the highest return, and OMX20 has the highest risk. All three assets have a positive slope. Danish mortgage bond has the steepest slope meaning for per unit risk-bearing it has the highest return. In the crisis (Figure 9-8), OMX20 shows a negative slope indicating that its excess return is minus. Gold still has the highest return, but the risk also rises. Overall Danish mortgage has the best return per unit risk no matter in the 2009 crisis or not. Gold is a preferable asset to stock as the stock has an unusual return below the free interest rate. Whereas, the Danish mortgage bond performs even better than the gold in crisis. Thus, in the portfolio of the general period, the bond is the major asset to invest. However, in the crisis, the percentage of investing in the bond is even bigger. On the other hand, the investment in gold in the portfolio is quite stable. No matter it is in the overall period or especially in the 2009 crisis, the proportion of gold is always around 7.2 % (Table 9-13 and Table 9-17). The actual volatility happens between the Danish mortgage bond and OMX20.

From the findings above, due to the extremely good performance of the Danish mortgage bond in the

2009 crisis, the portfolio of gold, stock, and bond have a better-expected return than usual. The risk, however, is almost the same. From the construction of the two portfolios, it can be confirmed that gold investment should keep a level at 7.2%. And no big change is necessary for the 2009 crisis period.

In the crisis

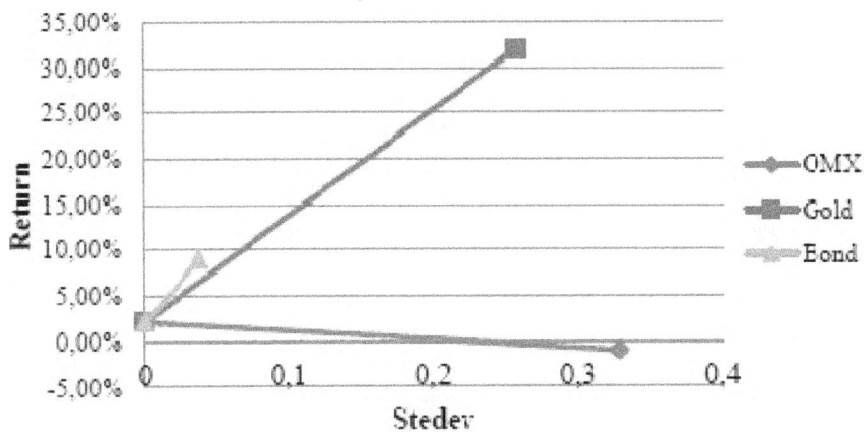

Figure 9-8 Assets performance in the crisis

Critique of the methods used in the project

In the process of writing this book, it is natural to face several issues in the analysis. Different assumptions have been made to solve the issues in the progress of conducting the paper. In the following section, we will address the assumptions made in the analysis to validate the analysis and in turn to give alternative solutions to the method used in the book. This will equally allow commenting on further studies that might extend the analysis of this book.

Is the selected data series sufficient?

The fundamental of the models in this book depends a lot on the quality of the data. It is important to use unbiased and normally distributed data. In Part Two, the monthly data collection of the gold's price, S&P 500, oil's price, U.S. interest rate, and U.S inflation rate from 1991 to 2011 is the largest in existence. Thus by using both Reuters Datastream Advance and the World Gold Council database the validity of the data is very high.

However, the model might not have sufficient explanatory power as the original model. The selected dataset might omit some important factors, which could better explain the return of gold. Though to fully explain the fluctuations in the return of gold is not the research question in this book, it could be another thesis to research that. The purpose has been to build an econometric model in SAS to identify some factors that affect the return on gold. Even some factors have been included, which proved irrelevant to the price of gold, it is still an achievement of the model to prove such a relationship.

In Part Three, three assets respectively stocks, gold, and bonds are chosen to construct portfolios. In the real world, an investment portfolio should contain more assets across the board than just OMX20, gold, and Danish mortgage bonds. Due to the scope of this book, only these three assets were selected in a portfolio to present a perspective of Danish investors. For future studies, it could be expanded to a more complicated portfolio including real estates, fixed income assets, and government bonds. The results can be compared with the institutional portfolios.

Risk-free rate

A risk-free rate of 4.09% has been used in the overall testing period from the 5th of January, 1993 to the 31st of August, 2011. A risk-free rate of 2.11% has been used in the 2009 crisis period from the 1st of October, 2008 to the 31st of August, 2011. The risk-free rate presented in this book is the 3-month Danish interbank rate. Alternatively, the risk-free rate can also be the interest rate on the Danish 10-year government bonds, an alternative that would have provided slight changes in the analysis.

Transaction cost

Since the gold, stocks, and bonds are very liquid assets, the transaction cost is therefore not subtracted from the return. All the transaction cost is assumed to be zero in this book. It can be questioned whether this assumption is correct or not. Transaction cost can be assumed different from zero, and then will be deducted from the return. Thus the calculated proportion of the portfolio in Part Three could be changed. But due to the small amounts in question, it would only give slight changes to the results in Part Three.

Before conclusion: Are the results from Part Two and Part Three realistic?

The return of gold has a positive correlation with the change in the inflation rate.

The result is not a surprise. As Figure 10-1 shows, the change in the price of gold has the same trend as the change in U.S. CPI. Governments and central banks hold gold as the backup of their existing currency because the value of gold (in terms of the real goods and services that it can buy) remains stable compared to the purchasing power of any paper currency. The change in the inflation rate reflects the increasing and decreasing purchasing power of the paper currency. Therefore when the currency has a low purchasing power, the price it can buy in gold will increase.

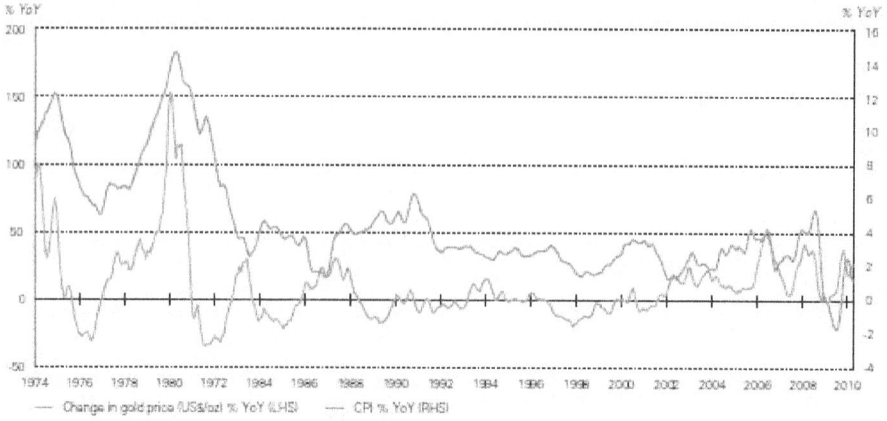

Figure 11-1 Change in the price of gold and change in US CPI, % year-on-year, three-month moving average

The return of gold does not correlate with the return of stocks

Stocks and gold do not have a direct link between each other. The result seems reasonable as no obvious reasoning is identified to explain the relationship between gold and stocks.

The return of gold has some positive correlation with the return of oil

The result that the return of gold has some positive correlation with the return of oil is not very strong. The test shows a result at the border-line, but it does indicate such a relationship. From history, however, such a positive correlation has happened. Between 1972 and 1974 when oil's prices tripled from $2.44 to $10.36, the price of gold also rose from $47.45 to $174.76 during the same period. Similarly, between 1978 and 1980, oil prices increased from $12.70 to $26.00, and the quarterly price of gold also increased from $178.33 to $631.40.

The recommended Portfolio with 3.57% invested in stocks, 7.2% invested in gold, and 89.23% invested in the Danish mortgage bond

The portfolio is calculated based on the daily returns, risks, and covariance among the different assets. The low risk and relatively high return make Danish mortgage bonds the most attractive. The issue is that the return is obtained in the period from 1993 to 2011, containing 4867 observations, which might not be large enough to capture an unbiased return. The 11.42% of OMX20 return seems reasonable as the world average stocks return is around 12%, whereas 9.81% of Danish mortgage bonds return is too good to be true. In reality, investors may expect lower returns on Danish mortgage bonds, and therefore the portfolio may include fewer Danish mortgage bonds.

The proportion of gold investment in the portfolio should not be adjusted in the period of the current crisis

Using the assumption that only the return and risk during the 2009 crisis period, which is from the 1st of October 2008 to the 31st of August 2011 is made to calculate the portfolio. The return of the portfolio in the crisis seems too good to be true, as it is even better than the normal portfolio return. However, the proportion of gold in the portfolio seems to be realistic.

Conclusion

Looking back from 2011, the past year is still under the impact of the crisis. Followed by the U.S. debt crisis, the European sovereign debt crisis prolongs the way of recovery. Due to fear of downgrading of government debt of certain European states and the negative return of stock markets, investing in gold, naturally, becomes popular again. This book is an academic paper of gold investments including the portfolio study. In conclusion, the findings from each part will be reported to construct a comprehensive investment recommendation.

Part Two of this book attempts to answer the research question: What are the relevant factors that affect the price of gold mostly? How they will influence the price of gold? To obtain the answer, several potential factors are identified. The most likely ones are selected before the testing. They are listed as the following: oil price index, S&P 500 index, U.S. interest rate, and U.S. inflation rate. Also, the relative data are collected, and the econometrical model is built, to test and report the findings.

The chosen testing period from January 1991 to August 2011, with monthly observations, shows that the return of gold has a strong positive correlation with the change of the inflation rate. The greater the rise of the inflation rate leads to the lower value of the paper currency. In the case of high inflation or the devaluation of paper currencies, people are more willing to hold gold as it has a static purchasing power to goods, and therefore the price of gold increased. The return of oil to some extent is positively related to the return of gold. However, they do not have a mirroring effect. The result in the test is on the border-line and while this shows a sign of the relationship, the evidence is not strong. The increasing number of observations is encouraged, as a testing period of 21 years might not be sufficient in identifying the relationship of the return movement.

The return of gold has also proven to not be related to the return of stocks or interest rates. The results of Part Two are carried on to Part Three. Since the return of gold is independent of the return of stocks, these two are put together in a portfolio to diversify the risk of each other.

Overall in Part Two, the most important two takeaways are that from the period of 1991 to 2011, the inflation rate is a factor that influences the price of gold. The change in the inflation rate has a positive effect on the return of the price of gold. And secondly, oil's price has a weaker positive effect on the price of gold. The stock and interest rates do not have any effect on the return of the price of gold.

Part Three of this book attempts to answer the research question: What are the annual returns and risks of gold investments in the last 20 years? How should an investor allocate his investment in a three-asset category portfolio, consisting of gold investment, stocks, and bonds in Denmark before and during the crisis? The calculation of return and risk shows that from the 5th of January 1993 to the 31st of August 2011, the annual return of gold is 12.64% with an 18.89% risk. The calculation of covariance shows that gold correlates almost zero to OMX20, which can create strong diversification by combining both in one portfolio. When calculating the portfolio of the investment the principle of maximizing the Sharpe ratio, to obtain the optimal portfolio with the highest return per unit risk, is applied. The tangent portfolio suggests that the proportion of gold and OMX20 should be 59.46% and 40.54% respectively. In the crisis, due to the negative performance of OMX20, gold should replace OMX20 in the portfolio.

Table 12-1 Result from Part Three

	Expected return	Risk
OMX20 20	11.43%	22.97%
Gold	12.64%	18.89%
Bond	9.81%	4.39%
Tangent portfolio	10.7%	4.27%

The result of the tangent portfolio of OMX20, Danish mortgage bonds, and gold are listed in Table 12-1. By holding 3.57% in OMX20, 7.20% in gold, and 89.23% in Danish mortgage bonds; one can obtain an optimal portfolio with the lowest risk and relatively high return. In the crisis, the proportion of investing in gold should remain the same. Bonds and OMX20 will have some small changes.

The very large proportion of bonds in the portfolio is because Danish mortgage bonds having a high yield and high security. Danish mortgage bonds have never defaulted in history. The result does not necessarily mean that bonds are safer than gold and stocks. They still have a risk of defaulting or being downgraded, especially under certain circumstances, such as when the housing bubble burst.

To have a comprehensive conclusion besides the recommended portfolio, it also needs to be addressed that gold is a very unique asset, which has a static purchasing power to goods and services in the long term. Adding gold to a portfolio can diversify the risks of stocks and bonds, and enhance the ability to bear risk in a crisis. The effect becomes significant when the risk of inflation and government default is prevalent.

Appendix 1 – The risk-free rate

The risk-free rate is obtained by taking the average of a 3-month Danish interbank rate from the corresponding period. Daily 3-month Danish interbank rate is downloaded from DataStream Advance 4.0. The average is calculated according to the modeling period.

Appendix 2 – Ways of investing in gold

A growing range of methods now allows investors to either buy gold or simply gain exposure to gold price movements. From gold coins, online accounts, exchange-traded funds, and complex financial products, to mining stocks, the most appropriate gold investments will depend upon the investor's specific requirements and outlook.

- **Coins and small bars**

King Croesus, ruler of the Kingdom of Lydia in western Asia Minor (latter-day Turkey) from 560 to 546BC, struck the first gold coins in history. The king minted gold brought from his mines and the sands of the River Pactolus. Gold coins have been a recognized form of legal tender ever since.

Bullion coins and small bars offer private investors an attractive way of investing in relatively small amounts of gold. In many countries - including the whole of the European Union - gold purchased for investment purposes is exempt from Value Added Tax.

Bullion coins

Investors can choose from a wide range of gold bullion coins, issued by governments across the world. In their country of issue, these coins are considered legal tender for their face value, rather than their gold content.

Alternatively, the market value of bullion coins is determined by their fine gold content, plus a premium or mark-up that varies between coins and dealers. Of course, the premium tends to be higher for smaller denominations.

Bullion coins may range in size from 1/20 ounce to 1000 grams, although the most common weights (in troy ounces of fine gold content) are 1/20, 1/10, 1/4, 1/2, and 1 ounce. It is important not to confuse bullion coins with commemorative or numismatic coins, whose value depends on their rarity, design, and finish rather than on their fine gold content. Many dealers sell both.

Small gold bars

Gold bars can be bought in a variety of weights and sizes, ranging from as little as one gram to 400 troy ounces (the size of the internationally traded London Good Delivery bar). The definition of a small bar is one that weighs 1000g or less.

According to industry specialists Gold Bars Worldwide, there are 110 accredited bar manufacturers and brands in 27 countries. Between them, they produce a total of more than 400 types of standard gold bars, all of which normally contain a minimum of 99.5% fine gold.

- **Exchange-Traded Funds (ETFs)**

Gold-backed Exchange Traded Funds (ETFs) and Exchange Traded Commodities (ETCs) are traded on a variety of stock exchanges around the globe. These regulated financial products are designed to provide investors with exposure to the price performance of spot gold bullion. Many of the currently available products are backed by gold bullion held in secure vaults. This is a principal distinction from derivative-based products that track the gold price, but which are not wholly-backed by physical gold bullion.

The largest of the physical gold bullion-backed ETFs is SPDR Gold Shares (GLD). Launched in 2004, GLD was the first such product to be made available in the US. Its primary listing is on the NYSE Arca. It was subsequently cross-listed on the Singapore Stock Exchange, the Hong Kong Stock Exchange, Bolsa Mexicana de Valores, and the Tokyo Stock Exchange.

ETFs, provide investors with a relatively cost-efficient and secure way to participate in the gold bullion market without the necessity of taking physical delivery of gold. By increasing investor understanding of the role gold plays within a balanced investment portfolio, ETFs have played a prominent role in establishing gold as a unique asset class.

Following the GLD launch, many more commodity ETFs have entered the market, which underscores the growing popularity of these products.

Financial advisors and other investment professionals can provide you with further details about gold-backed securities.

- **Futures and options**

Gold futures

Gold futures contracts are binding commitments to make or take delivery of a specified quantity and purity of gold, on a prescribed date, at an agreed price. The initial margin - or cash deposit paid to the broker - is only a fraction of the price of the gold underlying the contract.

That means investors can significantly leverage their investment. This can yield significant trading profits, and it can also cause equally significant losses in the event of an adverse movement in the gold price.

The key determining factor in futures prices is the market's perception of what the carrying costs ought to be at a given time. These include the interest cost of borrowing gold plus insurance and storage charges. The gold futures price is usually higher than the gold spot price.

Traders deal in futures contracts on regulated commodity exchanges. The largest of these is the New York Mercantile Exchange Comex Division (recently rebranded CME Globex, after a merger between Chicago Mercantile Exchange and NYMEX), the Chicago Board of Trade (part of CME), and the Tokyo Commodity Exchange. Gold futures also feature on exchanges in India and Dubai.

Tradable commodity indices, which are based on commodity futures, all include a small allocation to gold.

If you would like to find out more about gold futures, The Commodity Futures Trading Commission offers extensive reports on derivatives trading in the US.

Gold options

These give the holder the right, but not the obligation, to buy ('call' option) or sell ('put' option) a specified quantity of gold, at a predetermined price, by an agreed date. The cost of such an option depends on several factors, including the current spot price of gold, interest rates, anticipated or implied volatility, time to expiry, and of course the pre-agreed or 'strike price'.

A higher strike price will attract a less expensive

call option and a more expensive put option.

Like futures contracts, buying gold options can give the holder substantial leverage. Conveniently, where the strike price is not achieved, there is no obligation to exercise the option. That means the holder's loss is limited only to the premium paid for the option.

Like shares, both futures and options can be traded through brokers.

- **Warrants**

Leading investment banks commonly use gold warrants. These instruments give the buyer the right to buy gold at a specific price on a specific day in the future. For this right, the buyer pays a premium. Like futures, warrants are generally leveraged to the price of the underlying asset (in this case, gold). Gearing can also be on a one-for-one basis. In the past, gold warrants mostly applied to shares of gold mining companies.

- **Gold accounts**

Gold bullion banks offer two types of gold accounts - allocated and unallocated:

Allocated account

Similar to keeping gold in a safety deposit box, this is the most secure form of investment in physical gold. The gold is stored in a vault owned and managed by a recognized bullion dealer or depository.

Specific bars or coins are numbered and identified by hallmark, weight, and fineness. These are then allocated to each particular investor, who, in addition to the price of the gold, also pays the custodian for storage and insurance. The holder of gold in an allocated account has full ownership of that gold.

The bullion dealer or depository that owns the vault where the gold is stored may not trade, lease or lend the bars - except on the specific instructions of the account holder.

Unallocated account

Unallocated account investors do not have specific bars allotted to them (unless they take delivery of their gold, which they can usually do within two working days). Traditionally, one advantage of unallocated accounts has been the lack of any storage and insurance charges, because the bank reserves the right to lease the gold out.

Now that the gold lease rate is negative in real terms, some banks have begun to introduce charges even on unallocated accounts.

Of course, investors are exposed to the creditworthiness of the bank or dealer providing the service in the same way as they would be with any other kind of account.

As a general rule, bullion banks do not deal in quantities of less than 1000 ounces. Their customers are institutional investors, private banks acting on behalf of their clients, central banks, and gold market participants wishing to buy or borrow large quantities of gold.

Other opportunities for smaller investors include:

Gold pool accounts

There are alternative options for investors wishing to

open gold accounts of less than 1000 ounces. For instance, Gold Pool Accounts offer a defined, unsegmented interest in a Gold accounts pool of gold. You can invest in one of these accounts with as little as one ounce.

Electronic currencies

There are also various electronic 'currencies' available - linked to gold bullion in allocated storage. These offer a simple and cost-effective way of buying and selling gold and using it as money. Any amount of gold can be purchased, and these currencies allow gold to be used to send online payments worldwide.

- **Gold Accumulation Plans (GAP)**

Gold Accumulation Plans (GAPs) are similar to conventional savings plans in that they are based on the principle of putting aside a fixed sum of money every month. The fixed sum then buys gold every trading day in that month.

The fixed monthly sums can be small, and purchases are not subject to the premium normally charged on small bars or coins. Because small amounts of gold are bought over a long period, exposure to short term variations in price is contained.

At any time during the contract term (usually a minimum of a year), or when the account is closed, investors can get their gold in the form of bullion bars or coins, and sometimes even in the form of jewelry. Should they choose to sell their gold they can also get cash.

- **Gold Mining stocks**

Gold mining stocks are a popular way to gain exposure to gold and the opportunity for outperformance.

The gold mining sector is large and liquid. Over 300 gold mining companies are listed and publicly traded on various US stock exchanges alone. Globally the sector is capitalized at over US$220 billion. Capitalizations range from between US$50 – US$300 million to the large-cap gold mining stocks of over US$10 billion.

Investing in gold mining stocks is a logical substitute and complement to investing in other forms of physical gold. That's because the value of the stocks is driven significantly by the price of gold.

Also, the stock price is also impacted by the mines, projects, reserves of unmined gold below ground, or mining royalty income streams. Gold mining stocks do not simply track the price of gold in the same way that physical bullion, gold ETFs or gold futures do. These stocks are also a potential source of excess return or 'alpha' - over and above the return on gold.

Numerous factors are involved in the pricing and valuation of gold equities. These can include the maturity and geographic spread of mining projects, gold reserves, ore grades, costs, margins, profitability, and strength of balance sheet, the debt profile, and the quality of management. A combination of these forces will cause the share prices of gold stocks to act in a leveraged manner around the value of gold.

- **Gold Certificates**

Historically, the U.S. Treasury issued gold certificates from the civil war until 1933. Denominated in dollars, these certificates constituted part of the gold standard. Holders could exchange their gold certificates for an equal value of gold. Silver certificates later replaced gold certificates briefly, before giving way to Federal Reserve notes. U.S. Treasury gold certificates have been out of circulation for so long, they're now considered to be collectibles.

Today, gold certificates offer investors a method of holding gold without taking physical delivery. Individual banks, particularly in countries like Germany and Switzerland, issue these certificates. The paper confirms an individual's ownership, while the bank holds the metal on the client's behalf.

The client thus saves on storage and personal security issues. He or she also gains liquidity in terms of being able to sell portions of the holdings by simply telephoning the custodian.

The Perth Mint runs a certificate program that is guaranteed by the government of Western Australia and is distributed in several countries.

- **Gold orientated funds**

The term "collective investment vehicles" includes mutual funds open-ended investment companies (OEICs), closed-end funds, unit trusts, and any similar structures. A number of these vehicles specialize in the shares of gold mining companies and operate in various countries.

These funds are regulated financial products and therefore it is impossible to provide details on any specific funds here.

Funds usually differ in their structure. Some invest in shares of gold mining companies; others seek value in companies mining other minerals. Many funds will opt for a diverse approach, perhaps investing in futures and mining equities. Other funds may opt for a combination of gold mining equities as well as holdings of the underlying metal.

There are significant differences between an investment in a gold mining equity and a direct investment in gold bullion.

The appreciation potential of a gold mining company share depends on several factors. These include market expectations of the future price of gold, the costs of mining it, the likelihood of additional gold discoveries, and other factors. To a degree, the success of this type of investment depends on the future earnings and growth potential of the company.

Most gold mining equities tend to be more volatile than the gold price itself. In addition to being subject to the same risk factors as most other equities, there are additional risks linked to the mining industry in general - and to individual mining companies specifically.

- **Structured products**

Structured products usually hold a high minimum investment. For this reason, institutional investors dominate the market, along with gold market professionals in the case of forwards.

Forwards

Forward contracts are similar to futures. They are agreements to exchange an underlying asset
in this case, gold - at an agreed price, at a future date. They can be used to either manage risk or for speculative purposes.

Forwards and options trading on the over-the-counter (OTC) gold market differ significantly from futures or options that trade on one of the exchanges. Some of the key differences include:

- Counterparties will negotiate a forward contract (or OTC option) directly. The instrument is tailor-made, whereas futures contracts are standardized agreements that trade on an exchange.
- Although forward contracts offer the greater flexibility of a private agreement, they still pose a level of counterparty risk. Futures contracts carry

the guarantee of the exchange on which they trade and are therefore risk-free.

- The owner of a futures contract can sell to third parties at any point before maturity, making these instruments more liquid than forwarding contracts (whose obligations cannot be transferred).

Gold-linked bonds and structured notes

Gold-linked bonds are available from the world's largest bullion dealers and investment banks.

These products provide investors with a combination of:

- exposure to gold price fluctuations
- a yield
- principal protection.

Structured notes tend to allocate part of the sum invested in purchasing put/call options. The balance goes into traditional fixed income products, such as the money market, to generate a yield. Depending on the structure, they can offer capital protection and a varying degree of participation in price fluctuations. Naturally, the structure of the note will vary according to prevailing market conditions and personal investor preferences.

The distinction is not always clear between the purchase of physical gold and other investments that offer exposure to movements in the gold price. This is especially so as it has long been possible to invest in bullion without actually taking physical delivery.

If you are considering an investment in gold, it is important to appraise yourself of the best options for your specific needs. The following questions are designed to help you decide on the channel or channels of gold investment that is most appropriate for you.

- Why did you decide to buy gold?
- Do you want a real asset that is physically available at all times or do you simply want exposure to the gold price?
- Will you want the gold delivered to you or would you prefer it to be stored in a vault?
- Do you have information about all the costs that may be involved? These include taxes, commissions, premiums, storage, and insurance.
- Is the counterparty (i.e. the person or company from or through whom you will be making the purchase) reliable and trustworthy?

- How does gold fit in with your other investments?

Appendix 3 - London Gold Fixing Price

The London gold fixing takes place twice daily over the telephone and sets a price at which all known orders to buy and sell gold on a spot basis at the time of the fix can be settled. The fix is widely used as the benchmark for spot transactions throughout the market. The five members of the fix 'meet' at 10:30 and 3:00 London time and commence the fix with a trying price. The fixing members' representatives relay the price down to their dealing rooms, who are in contact with as many bullion dealers as are interested (or who have interested clients) and these market members then declare how much metal, on a net basis, they require buying or selling at that level. The dealers are themselves in contact with their clients, who may change their order, or add or cancel an order, at any time. The position declared by the dealers is the net position outstanding between all their clients (i.e. if one bank has clients wanting to buy a total of two tonnes, and other clients wanting to sell a total of one tonne, then he declares himself as a buyer of one tonne). Each fixing member then nets off the position and declares himself, as the representative of all those interested parties, as a net buyer or seller (and of how much), or to be in balance. If the market is out of balance with more gold required than offered, then the price will be adjusted upwards (and vice versa) until the balance is achieved (because some clients will withdraw or amend their orders if the price does not suit them). At this point, the price is declared fixed. On very rare occasions the price will be fixed when there is an imbalance, at the discretion of the chairman of the fix. The fix is thus entirely open and any market user may participate through his bank.

Appendix 4 - Scatter plot for data series

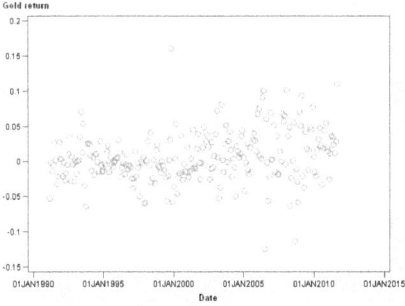

Gold return

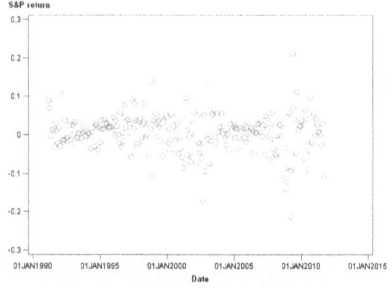

S&P return

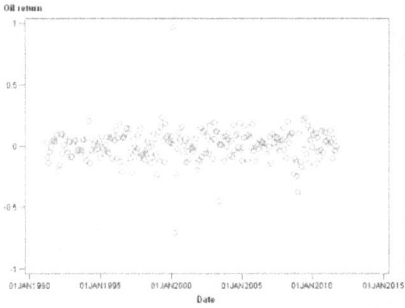

Oil return

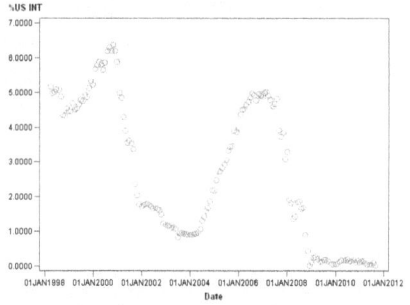

%US INT

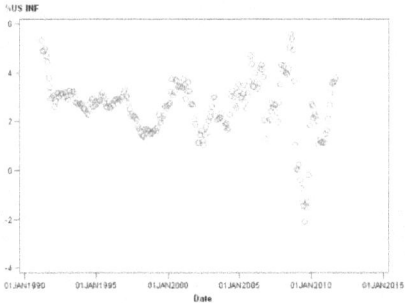

%US INF

Appendix 5 - ADF tests for LN data series

Name of Variable = LN Gold price

			Autocorrelation Check for White Noise						
To Lag	Chi-Square	DF	Pr > ChiSq	Autocorrelations					
6	1344.88	6	<.0001	0.980	0.963	0.946	0.930	0.913	0.896
12	2452.29	12	<.0001	0.881	0.865	0.849	0.833	0.816	0.800
18	3348.41	18	<.0001	0.785	0.770	0.754	0.739	0.723	0.709
24	4053.23	24	<.0001	0.694	0.678	0.662	0.645	0.629	0.614

Augmented Dickey-Fuller Unit Root Tests							
Type	Lags	Rho	Pr < Rho	Tau	Pr < Tau	F	Pr > F
Zero Mean	0	0.2714	0.7476	2.98	0.9993		
	1	0.2697	0.7471	2.64	0.9981		
	2	0.2770	0.7490	2.96	0.9993		
Single Mean	0	3.4683	0.9998	2.97	0.9999	8.33	0.0010
	1	3.4180	0.9998	2.69	0.9999	6.67	0.0010
	2	3.4603	0.9998	3.05	0.9999	8.51	0.0010
Trend	0	0.4710	0.9978	0.28	0.9984	7.35	0.0229
	1	0.2473	0.9971	0.14	0.9975	6.55	0.0441
	2	0.7539	0.9985	0.48	0.9992	7.51	0.0197

Trend and Correlation Analysis for LN Gold price

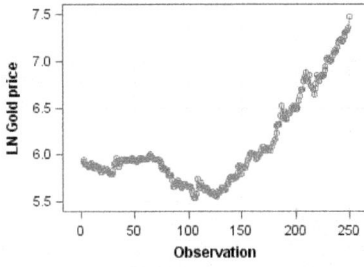

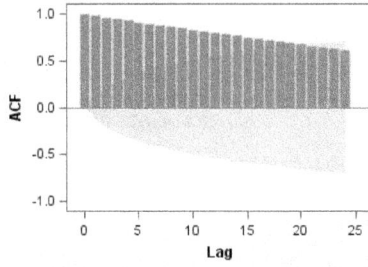

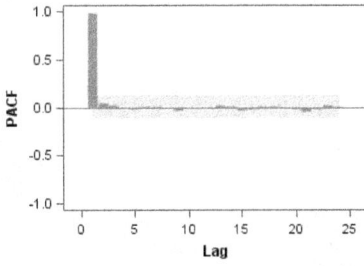

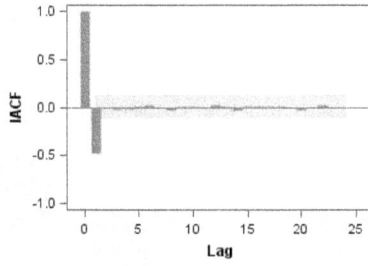

ARIMA Modeling and Forecasting
Results
The ARIMA Procedure

To Lag	Chi-Square	DF	Pr > ChiSq	Autocorrelations					
6	1355.45	6	<.0001	0.983	0.955	0.950	0.934	0.917	0.900
12	2464.78	12	<.0001	0.884	0.857	0.849	0.833	0.816	0.799
18	3347.39	18	<.0001	0.781	0.756	0.750	0.734	0.716	0.700
24	4019.07	24	<.0001	0.682	0.654	0.646	0.629	0.611	0.595

Autocorrelation Check for White Noise

Augmented Dickey-Fuller Unit Root Tests

Type	Lags	Rho	Pr < Rho	Tau	Pr < Tau	F	Pr > F
Zero Mean	0	0.1734	0.7232	1.55	0.9707		
	1	0.1772	0.7241	1.61	0.9737		
	2	0.1662	0.7214	1.51	0.9681		
Single Mean	0	-3.6932	0.5720	-2.19	0.2111	3.86	0.0968
	1	-3.8427	0.5547	-2.31	0.1690	4.25	0.0732
	2	-3.4399	0.6018	-2.08	0.2525	3.55	0.1661
Trend	0	-4.1862	0.8739	-1.51	0.8240	2.41	0.6963
	1	-4.2533	0.8597	-1.56	0.8053	2.68	0.6422
	2	-3.7712	0.8984	-1.40	0.8595	2.17	0.7446

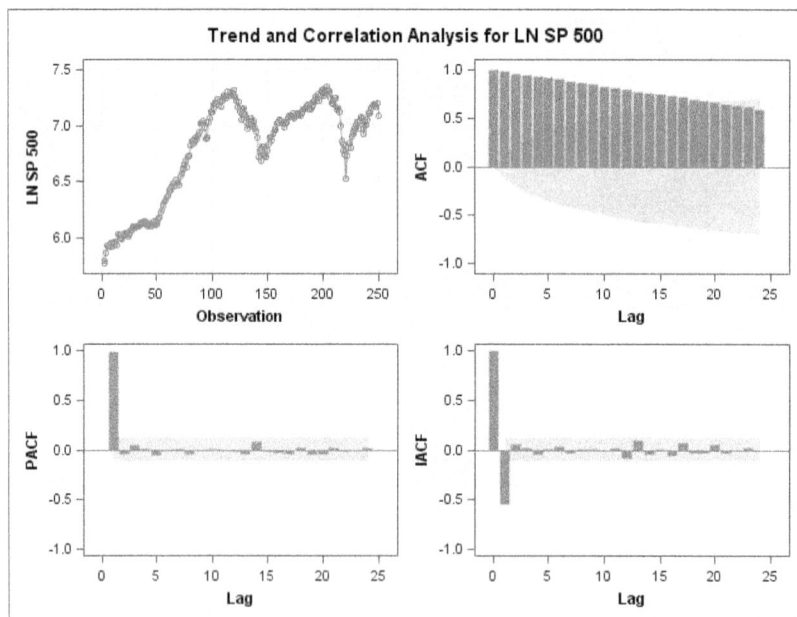

Trend and Correlation Analysis for LN SP 500

ARIMA Modeling and Forecasting
Results
The ARIMA Procedure

Name of Variable = LN Oil

To Lag	Chi-Square	DF	Pr > ChiSq	Autocorrelations					
6	1293.89	6	<.0001	0.972	0.950	0.930	0.911	0.889	0.867
12	2310.98	12	<.0001	0.849	0.829	0.814	0.799	0.781	0.762
18	3139.16	18	<.0001	0.745	0.732	0.724	0.714	0.703	0.691
24	3857.68	24	<.0001	0.685	0.673	0.664	0.653	0.646	0.640

Autocorrelation Check for White Noise

Type	Lags	Rho	Pr < Rho	Tau	Pr < Tau	F	Pr > F
Zero Mean	0	0.2093	0.7320	0.47	0.8154		
	1	0.2716	0.7476	0.72	0.8701		
	2	0.2783	0.7493	0.78	0.8810		
Single Mean	0	-3.4919	0.5956	-1.07	0.7266	0.77	0.8746
	1	-2.0543	0.7711	-0.74	0.8337	0.62	0.9166
	2	-1.6627	0.8169	-0.62	0.8615	0.58	0.9296
Trend	0	-22.0745	0.0413	-3.65	0.0279	7.12	0.0286
	1	-16.5843	0.1297	-3.07	0.1160	5.18	0.1414
	2	-15.9522	0.1469	-2.99	0.1359	5.02	0.1738

Augmented Dickey-Fuller Unit Root Tests

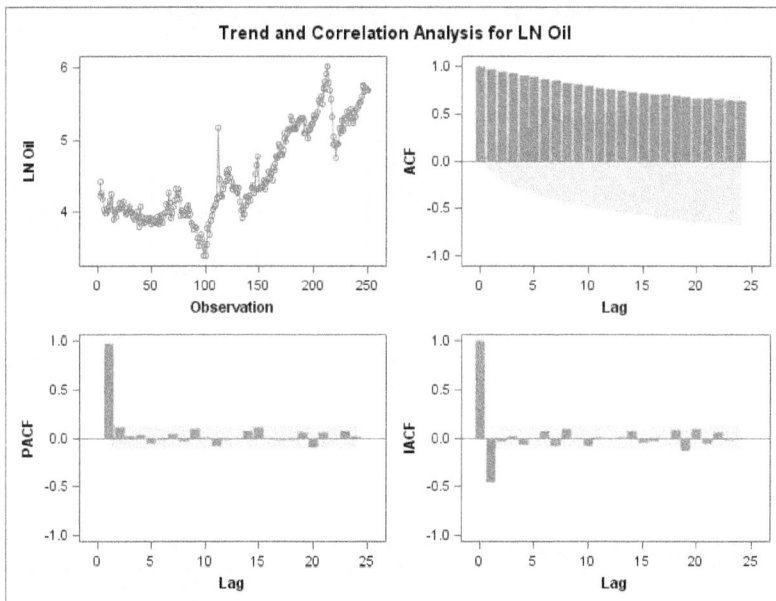

Trend and Correlation Analysis for LN Oil

Appendix 6 - ADF Test for Return Data Series

Name of Variable = Gold return

Autocorrelation Check for White Noise									
To Lag	Chi-Square	DF	Pr > ChiSq	Autocorrelations					
6	7.25	6	0.2981	0.098	-0.078	0.035	0.106	-0.023	0.015
12	17.90	12	0.1187	0.056	0.024	0.004	0.049	0.187	0.004
18	21.50	18	0.2548	-0.030	0.014	0.064	0.060	0.047	0.050
24	33.15	24	0.1009	0.002	0.141	0.058	0.113	0.055	0.060

Augmented Dickey-Fuller Unit Root Tests							
Type	Lags	Rho	Pr < Rho	Tau	Pr < Tau	F	Pr > F
Zero Mean	0	-214.380	0.0001	-13.55	<.0001		
	1	-243.450	0.0001	-10.74	<.0001		
	2	-192.481	0.0001	-8.05	<.0001		
Single Mean	0	-220.937	0.0001	-13.93	<.0001	97.09	0.0010
	1	-264.245	0.0001	-11.21	<.0001	62.92	0.0010
	2	-225.275	0.0001	-8.54	<.0001	36.52	0.0010
Trend	0	-233.342	0.0001	-14.65	<.0001	107.32	0.0010
	1	-309.404	0.0001	-12.16	<.0001	73.97	0.0010
	2	-310.715	0.0001	-9.51	<.0001	45.24	0.0010

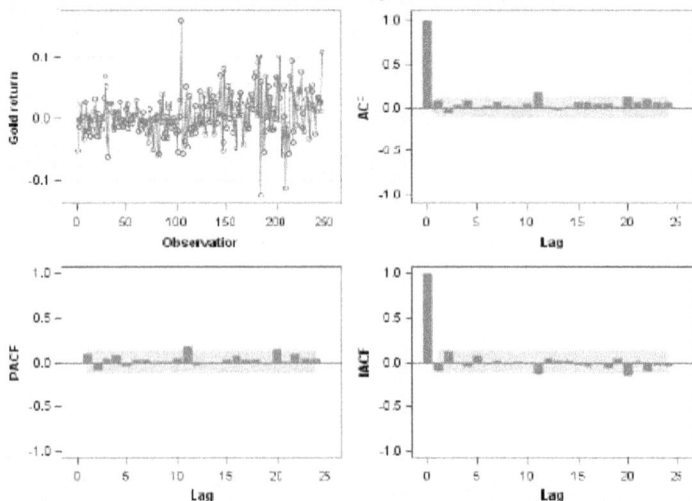

Trend and Correlation Analysis for Gold return

ARIMA Modeling and Forecasting
Results
The ARIMA Procedure

To Lag	Chi-Square	DF	Pr > ChiSq	Autocorrelations					
6	8.29	6	0.2179	-0.167	-0.032	-0.037	0.032	0.007	-0.040
12	16.88	12	0.1540	0.056	-0.129	0.026	0.101	0.019	-0.048
18	24.35	18	0.1440	-0.081	-0.107	-0.001	0.019	0.025	-0.095
24	33.18	24	0.1003	0.110	-0.061	0.040	-0.066	0.001	-0.103

Autocorrelation Check for White Noise

Type	Lags	Rho	Pr < Rho	Tau	Pr < Tau	F	Pr > F
Zero Mean	0	-286.601	0.0001	-18.49	<.0001		
	1	-320.709	0.0001	-12.62	<.0001		
	2	-381.128	0.0001	-10.33	<.0001		
Single Mean	0	-287.191	0.0001	-18.50	<.0001	171.10	0.0010
	1	-323.514	0.0001	-12.65	<.0001	79.99	0.0010
	2	-390.414	0.0001	-10.39	<.0001	53.93	0.0010
Trend	0	-287.940	0.0001	-18.52	<.0001	171.48	0.0010
	1	-326.812	0.0001	-12.68	<.0001	80.40	0.0010
	2	-399.320	0.0001	-10.41	<.0001	54.25	0.0010

Augmented Dickey-Fuller Unit Root Tests

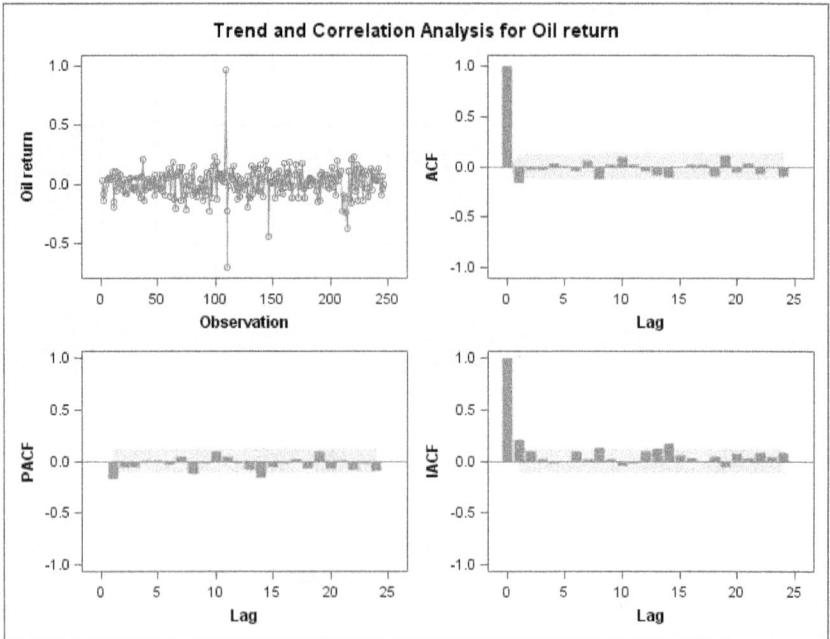

Trend and Correlation Analysis for Oil return

ARIMA Modeling and Forecasting
Results
The ARIMA Procedure

Name of Variable = SP return

| | Autocorrelation Check for White Noise | | | | | | | | |

To Lag	Chi-Square	DF	Pr > ChiSq	Autocorrelations					
6	5.79	6	0.4477	-0.015	-0.009	0.038	0.130	0.031	-0.056
12	11.16	12	0.5156	0.045	0.063	-0.049	-0.032	0.097	0.043
18	17.96	18	0.4581	-0.052	-0.051	0.008	0.095	-0.055	0.090
24	20.86	24	0.6469	0.069	-0.062	-0.020	-0.035	-0.018	0.007

Augmented Dickey-Fuller Unit Root Tests							
Type	Lags	Rho	Pr < Rho	Tau	Pr < Tau	F	Pr > F
Zero Mean	0	-246.596	0.0001	-15.64	<.0001		
	1	-247.097	0.0001	-11.13	<.0001		
	2	-212.259	0.0001	-8.55	<.0001		
Single Mean	0	-249.741	0.0001	-15.78	<.0001	124.47	0.0010
	1	-256.019	0.0001	-11.27	<.0001	63.57	0.0010
	2	-226.870	0.0001	-8.69	<.0001	37.82	0.0010
Trend	0	-251.936	0.0001	-15.89	<.0001	126.25	0.0010
	1	-262.321	0.0001	-11.38	<.0001	64.77	0.0010
	2	-237.455	0.0001	-8.82	<.0001	38.86	0.0010

Trend and Correlation Analysis for SP return

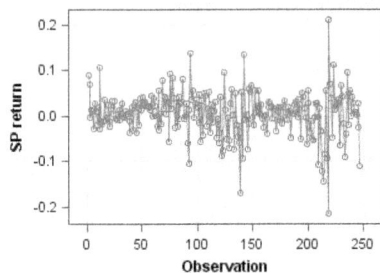

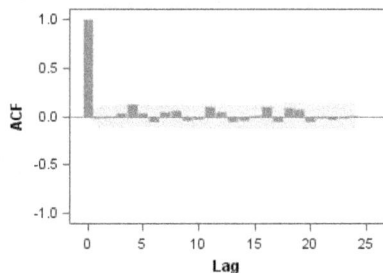

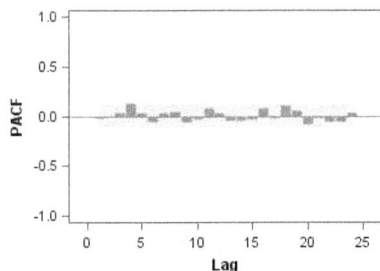

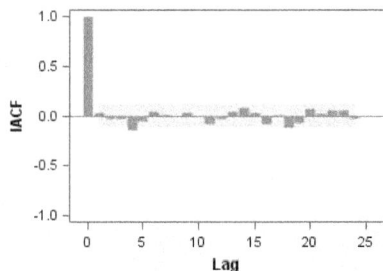

Appendix 7 - ADF test for delta US Inflation rate and US Interest rate

ARIMA Modeling and Forecasting

Results

The ARIMA Procedure

Name of Variable = delta US INF%

				Autocorrelation Check for White Noise					
To Lag	Chi-Square	DF	Pr > ChiSq	Autocorrelations					
6	41.21	6	<.0001	0.393	-0.026	-0.049	0.001	-0.077	-0.035
12	116.92	12	<.0001	0.006	-0.045	-0.022	0.077	-0.036	-0.529
18	173.90	18	<.0001	-0.379	-0.037	0.169	0.151	0.127	0.057
24	184.54	24	<.0001	0.038	-0.012	-0.022	-0.080	-0.174	0.012

			Augmented Dickey-Fuller Unit Root Tests				
Type	Lags	Rho	Pr < Rho	Tau	Pr < Tau	F	Pr > F
Zero Mean	0	-149.259	<.0001	-10.34	<.0001		
	1	-229.373	0.0001	-10.70	<.0001		
	2	-193.005	0.0001	-8.27	<.0001		
Single Mean	0	-149.294	0.0013	-10.32	<.0001	53.28	0.0010
	1	-229.469	0.0001	-10.68	<.0001	57.03	0.0010
	2	-193.151	0.0001	-8.26	<.0001	34.10	0.0010
Trend	0	-149.938	0.0005	-10.33	<.0001	53.36	0.0010
	1	-231.362	0.0001	-10.70	<.0001	57.20	0.0010
	2	-196.057	0.0001	-8.28	<.0001	34.31	0.0010

Trend and Correlation Analysis for delta US INF%

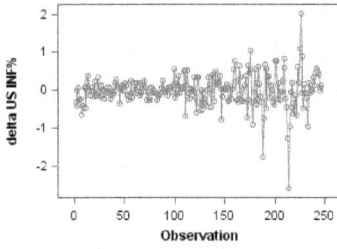

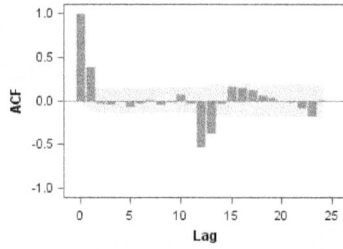

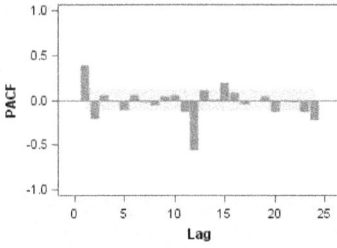

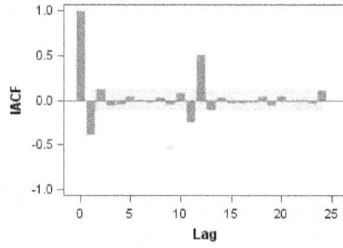

ARIMA Modeling and Forecasting
Results
The ARIMA Procedure

To Lag	Chi-Square	DF	Pr > ChiSq	Autocorrelations					
6	62.29	6	<.0001	0.228	0.282	0.188	0.090	0.198	0.182
12	102.00	12	<.0001	0.119	0.319	0.166	0.068	0.041	0.066
18	102.79	18	<.0001	-0.021	-0.034	-0.034	-0.000	-0.015	0.006
24	115.48	24	<.0001	-0.106	-0.065	-0.037	-0.157	-0.067	-0.026

Autocorrelation Check for White Noise

Type	Lags	Rho	Pr < Rho	Tau	Pr < Tau	F	Pr > F
Zero Mean	0	-187.724	0.0001	-12.31	<.0001		
	1	-113.176	0.0001	-7.54	<.0001		
	2	-89.4779	<.0001	-6.17	<.0001		
Single Mean	0	-189.901	0.0001	-12.39	<.0001	76.82	0.0010
	1	-115.599	0.0001	-7.59	<.0001	28.84	0.0010
	2	-91.9521	0.0015	-6.22	<.0001	19.33	0.0010
Trend	0	-189.925	0.0001	-12.37	<.0001	76.53	0.0010
	1	-115.677	0.0001	-7.58	<.0001	28.77	0.0010
	2	-92.0854	0.0006	-6.21	<.0001	19.31	0.0010

Augmented Dickey-Fuller Unit Root Tests

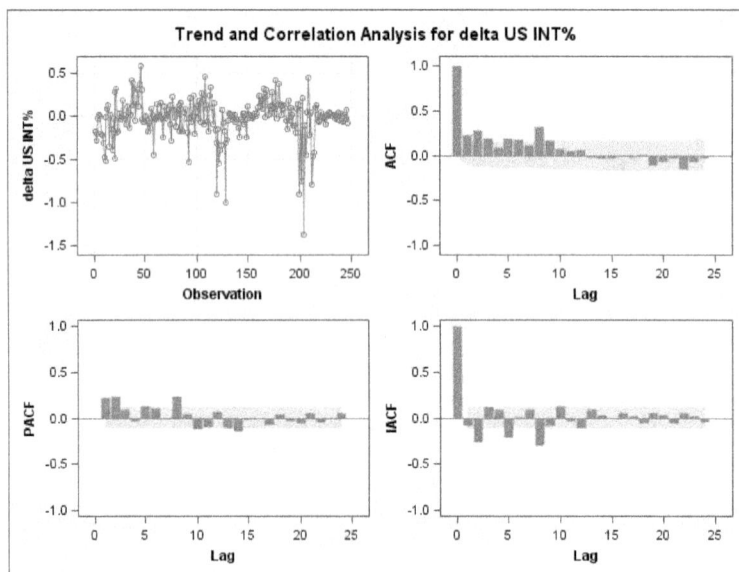

Trend and Correlation Analysis for delta US INT%

Appendix 8 - Macro Function of Conducting Covariance Matrix in Excel

```
Function VarCovar(rng As Range) As Variant
Dim i As Integer
Dim j As Integer
Dim numCols As Integer
numCols = rng.Columns.Count
Dim matrix() As Double
ReDim matrix(numCols - 1, numCols - 1)

For i = 1 To numCols
For j = 1 To numCols
matrix(I - 1, j - 1) =
Application.WorksheetFunction.Covar(rng.Columns(i),
rng.Columns(j))
Next j
Next i
VarCovar = matrix
End Function
```

Appendix 9 - Efficient Frontier and CML of Two Assets from the Overall Period

Efficient Frontier - 2 Assets – Overall Period						
	-17	-16,3	-15,6	-14,9	-14,2	-13,5	-12,8
OMX20	0,997382	0,973006	0,94863	0,924254	0,899879	0,875503	0,851127
Gold Price	0,002601	0,0269777	0,051354	0,075731	0,100107	0,124484	0,14886
Mean	0,114291	0,1145862	0,114882	0,115177	0,115472	0,115768	0,116063
Variance	0,05245	0,0499032	0,047463	0,04513	0,042904	0,040785	0,038773
Stdev	0,229021	0,2233902	0,21786	0,212438	0,207133	0,201953	0,19691
	-12,1	-11,4	-10,7	-10	-9,3	-8,6	-7,9
OMX20	0,826751	0,8023755	0,778	0,753624	0,729248	0,704872	0,680497
Gold Price	0,173237	0,1976131	0,22199	0,246366	0,270743	0,295119	0,319495
Mean	0,116358	0,1166539	0,116949	0,117245	0,11754	0,117835	0,118131
Variance	0,036869	0,0350711	0,033381	0,031797	0,030321	0,028952	0,02769
Stdev	0,192012	0,1872728	0,182704	0,178318	0,174129	0,170152	0,166402
	-7,2	-6,5	-5,8	-5,1	-4,4	-3,7	-3
OMX20	0,656121	0,6317451	0,607369	0,582994	0,558618	0,534242	0,509866
Gold Price	0,343872	0,3682484	0,392625	0,417001	0,441378	0,465754	0,490131
Mean	0,118426	0,1187215	0,119017	0,119312	0,119608	0,119903	0,120198
Variance	0,026535	0,0254866	0,024546	0,023712	0,022985	0,022366	0,021853
Stdev	0,162894	0,1596452	0,156671	0,153987	0,151609	0,149552	0,147828
	-2,3	-1,6	-0,9	-0,2	0,5	1,2	1,9
OMX20	0,48549	0,4611147	0,436739	0,412363	0,387987	0,363612	0,339236
Gold Price	0,514507	0,5388837	0,56326	0,587637	0,612013	0,63639	0,660766

Mean	0,120494	0,1207891	0,121085	0,12138	0,121675	0,121971	0,122266
Variance	0,021448	0,0211496	0,020958	0,020874	0,020897	0,021027	0,021264
Stdev	0,146451	0,1454289	0,14477	0,144479	0,144559	0,145008	0,145823
	2,6	3,3	4	4,7	5,4	6,1	6,8
OMX20	0,31486	0,2904842	0,266108	0,241733	0,217357	0,192981	0,168605
Gold Price	0,685143	0,7095191	0,733896	0,758272	0,782649	0,807025	0,831401
Mean	0,122561	0,1228568	0,123152	0,123448	0,123743	0,124038	0,124334
Variance	0,021609	0,0220601	0,022618	0,023284	0,024057	0,024936	0,025923

Stdev	0,146999	0,1485263	0,150394	0,152591	0,155102	0,157912	0,161007
	7,5	8,2	8,9	9,6	10,3	11	
OMX20	0,14423	0,1198538	0,095478	0,071102	0,046726	0,022351	
Gold Price	0,855778	0,8801544	0,904531	0,928907	0,953284	0,97766	
Mean	0,124629	0,1249244	0,12522	0,125515	0,125811	0,126106	
Variance	0,027017	0,028218	0,029526	0,030941	0,032464	0,034093	
Stdev	0,164369	0,1679823	0,171832	0,175901	0,180176	0,184643	

CML - 2 Assets Overall period			
	Risk-Free	Tangent	Outsider
Mean	4,09%	12,19%	0,162395
Variance	0	0,02097920	
Stdev	0	14,484%	21,726%

CPSIA information can be obtained
at www.ICGtesting.com
Printed in the USA
BVHW061554261020
591850BV00012B/993

9 781801 133388